A LOGO FOR LONDON

THE LONDON TRANSPORT
BAR AND CIRCLE

DAVID LAWRENCE

with preface and foreword by

MIKE BROWN, MVO
Managing Director, London Underground Limited

DAVID WORTHINGTON
Trustee, London Transport Museum

Laurence King Publishing
in association with the London Transport Museum

For Leila and for Jim

LAURENCE KING

Published in 2013 by
Laurence King Publishing Ltd
361–373 City Road
London EC1V 1LR
United Kingdom
email: enquiries@laurenceking.com
www.laurenceking.com

A catalogue record for this book is available from the British Library

ISBN: 978-1-78067-296-0

Design by David Pearson and Nicky Barneby

Printed in China

FRONTISPIECE: 'Signs that signify service', poster by Hans Arnold Rothholz and the Gordon Lawrence Studio, 1946.

CONTENTS

PREFACE

When one thinks of London, there are a few images that immediately spring to mind: the red double-decker bus, the phone box or post box, perhaps Buckingham Palace, Tower Bridge, or even – in the modern age – the London Eye or the Olympic Stadium. Few icons, however, sum up London as completely as the roundel. Outside Underground stations, in its most famous form of blue and red, the roundel brings a sense of continuity and consistency to a rapidly changing city and world.

The roundel first appeared on London Underground platforms in 1908 as a station nameplate. The idea was straightforward: this consistent and distinct shape would allow passengers to pick out the station name more easily from the midst of advertising and other poster information on display. Developed over time, the symbol still serves this vital purpose throughout our system.

By 1919 Frank Pick's vision and Edward Johnston's 'Underground' typeface had combined to created the roundel we know today. Transport in London now would be unrecognizable to our Victorian forefathers but, unlike aviation, retail or other businesses whose brands change with confusing regularity, the symbol for London's transport network has prevailed. Looking at old photographs of central London, or of the high streets of the many towns and villages which make up the greater metropolis, there have been many changes over the last century. Small shops and businesses are replaced by chain stores and tall offices; modern buses, cars and lorries have replaced horse-drawn vehicles and trams, and what people wear has transformed down the decades. Even those rare brands seen on the gable walls of old buildings that have survived the test of time have different logos and styles.

But the one consistent feature in many old photos is the 'bar and circle' of London Transport. Of course, it has evolved and been presented in many formats and colour schemes over the years, but it remains instantly familiar as a logo representative of progress and innovation, as well as a continuing and formidable service ethos. The roundel is an indelible icon across the city of London, and this book is a welcome and valuable contribution to the heritage and continued vibrancy of London Underground and Transport for London as a whole.

MIKE BROWN, MVO
Managing Director, London Underground Limited

FOREWORD

Human beings have always been familiar with iconography. Branding is not a new idea: it has communicated friend or foe, safety or danger, from the first time someone ate a poisonous berry or was stung by a wasp.

Yellow and black together signify danger; stripes make things disappear or tell us to stay clear; spots warn of problems; red indicates caution, green that we are good to go. The conversion of this visual language to man-made symbols is unsurprising, and there are hundreds of notable examples: the Olympic rings, the Red Cross, the Christian cross, the golden arches of McDonald's and the shell of Shell. Often these devices represent a set of beliefs, frequently the ideology of something better; sometimes they codify membership and in modern parlance they nearly always provide a short-hand for apparent quality.

London's simple icon of a bar and circle is no different; whether covering the side of a building or reproduced smaller than a fingernail, the practical and emotional messages contained within have made it one of the most enduring marques. The roundel, as it is officially known (the London Underground logo to you and me), reflects and represents nearly 100 years of the history of London as a capital city. The subtle shifts and changes in its form are recognised and understood by graphic designers, art workers and printers, who can provide date-accurate rationale and commentary as to how and why it has changed.

Yet strangely, even if you are not a design professional and don't understand the precise version of the logo you are looking at, somehow you too can have a reasonable idea of its date and describe what London was like at the time; and if you were there you can describe what you were doing, where you lived and who you hung out with. And so it is that this remarkable book helps to make sense of living in London, because as you unpack the history of this tiny piece of insignia, you find yourself unpacking the history of your own sense of place in this city.

The title of Norman Collins's wonderful novel *London Belongs to Me* sums it up: the London Underground logo belongs to me too. It's a marker for the London I know and love, the moniker that sets London apart from any other capital city and the symbol of the time London and I will spend together, whether for a weekend or a lifetime.

DAVID WORTHINGTON
Trustee, London Transport Museum

LONDON TRANSPORT

UNDERGROUND

BUSES

TROLLEYBUSES

TRAMS

FOR TRAFFIC ENQUIRIES

PHONE
ABB 1234

OR

WRITE
PUBLIC
ENQUIRIES
55 BROADWAY
S.W.1

ECKERSLEY 44

WATERLOW & SONS LIMITED, LONDON & DUNSTABLE.

INTRODUCTION

This is the story of a much-admired, and emulated, design – the London Transport symbol. It is composed of a circle or ring, across which a rectangular bar is inscribed; colour the circle or the bar, or both, label it with text or leave it plain, this is one of the best-known brands of the modern era, 'summing up . . . a very distinguished tradition of service and design'.[2] It does not actually symbolize anything pictorially or typographically, but it identifies, it informs and it decorates – that is its essential, useful beauty. In this book, arranged by theme over a chronological framework, we will see how the bar and circle – formerly called the Underground or London Transport bulls-eye, and presently the Transport for London roundel – achieved its status as a travel and cultural icon.

A sign or symbol is a recognizable mark that conveys an understood meaning. It can refer to something practical and visible, or abstract and unseen; it can indicate a single entity or activity, or a whole collection of related ideas and intentions. Heraldic arms, the flags of nations and insignia of businesses are obvious examples of signs and symbols, as are airline liveries, uniforms, product trademarks, fuel-company logos and fashion brands. These signs or symbols can utilize colour, shape, text or pattern in their design. They may also be rendered three-dimensionally, and in many different materials and scales.

Organizations form themselves around symbols. Whether using fundamental marks such as the Christian cross, flags, uniforms, armorial bearings, liveries or brands, collective groupings are identified by signs and symbols. Straightforward and simple symbols are very effective at communicating an organizational identity to the outside world. Other brand devices are more subtle and 'of their time', and correspond to changing attitudes about the way design can reflect the aspirations and values of a business. There are many failed brands which are testament to bad design or misguided strategy, and there are many brands which have come to be products in their own right, effecting the sale of merchandise or services on the basis of the reputation or lifestyle implied by

'Design is not a mode that enters in here and there and may be omitted elsewhere. Design must enter everywhere.'
FRANK PICK[1]

OPPOSITE: 'For traffic enquiries', poster by Tom Eckersley, 1944.

9

the brand identity. Victorian railway entrepreneurs commissioned coats of arms to embellish their locomotives and publicity, and to allay the concerns of travellers by giving authority and longevity to a new and potentially frightening technology. The bar and circle was central to the transformation of one of the first underground rail networks from a British Victorian railway into a modern urban transportation system based on European and North American practices of operation and promotion.

A TOTAL BRAND

In 2013 the oldest part of the London Underground has been in service for 150 years, and the organization which created the major part of the city's transport infrastructure was founded 80 years ago. Within two decades of the first fully underground railway opening in London, the operating company had developed a brand that has remained in use for over a century, and which now represents almost all the transport modes in the capital. A brand is used to promote an organization, to announce its presence and activities, to unify its operations and to present its best and most positive 'face' to the world at large. When it works well, the brand defines the personality of the organization.

The bar and circle began as a way of identifying railway station platforms to travellers, and of indicating the organization behind London's largest fleet of buses and its operating staff. Many leading craftspeople, designers and architects of the twentieth century are closely associated with the symbol. Edward Johnston, Edward McKnight Kauffer, Charles Holden, Tom Eckersley, Abram Games, Hans Schleger and Misha Black all worked alongside a team of enlightened amateurs and civil servants. It became an important part of a pioneering project to develop a total brand identity for business use. It was unusual, and all the more special, in representing a complex network of transportation and supporting services.

The symbol developed rapidly to be used to identify every part of the network, so that early in the twentieth century it was incorporated into the newly developed art of graphic design for publicity posters, and into the emerging fields of industrial design and modern architecture. London Transport's symbol was already established as a sophisticated and confident brand mark when airlines and motor-car manufacturers began to realize the potential of corporate identity in the 1930s. By the 1950s, as corporations that knew their business were searching out corporate-identity consultants, London Transport was a worldwide example of innovation and success in the practice of total design, crafting every aspect of its operations to ensure that they were in harmony and with a common visual message. Over the ensuing decades, the form and use of the logo has evolved and been adapted by its owners across every medium, from website to buildings, and it has survived redesign and more than one potential withdrawal. Its current phase of creating a family of symbols for different transport modes is exemplary for its clarity and consistency, and for being universally recognizable.

FORM

The bar and circle is a simple but clever shape with two geometric components. The most straightforward explanation for the bar across the symbol is that for centuries it has been the simplest framing method for written text – be it a clay tablet, a stone inscription or a printed label. On the railway systems of the world, it formed the obvious, if not ubiquitous, means of announcing to travellers the names of the stopping places, and giving railway workers the geographical location of infrastructure elements.

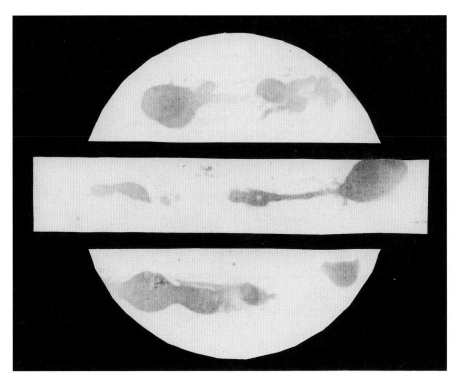

Impression of the original Underground bar-and-disc symbol from a design of 1908, recreated in 1955 by former Underground officer W.H. Hilton.

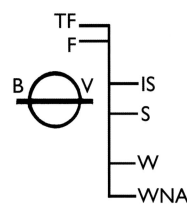

The Plimsoll load line.

When the first humans drew the sun, they inscribed a circle. When they sought to build and travel, objects with a circular form proved the most efficient aids. Direction finding produced circular compasses, and science called for circular lenses. Looking into the sky through these lenses, astronomers followed the ancients by drawing circular symbols for several planets and their positions: the sun's centre is shown as a circle horizontally bisected by a line. As a wheel, the circle symbolizes eternity and good luck; it appears in alchemy and magic. Given wings it traditionally represents safe travel, and has been used in this form for many transportation emblems.

And so we arrive at the idea of a bar and circle as a sign. A leading promoter of the bar and circle for London's Underground Group of companies was Frank Pick, and he is said to have noted the maritime Plimsoll load line symbol as an inspiration for his organization's trade mark.[3] The bar and circle was attributed by one leading art historian as representing London crossed by the underground railway.[4] Subsequently the disc would become a ring, and once established in this form the symbol was adopted throughout the Underground Group's public manifestations. This functioned in exactly the same way as advertising in 1900 as it does today – the relentless and crafted repetition of the same sign in essentially the same form across a multitude of uses. The symbol works as a positive shape – in single colours and combinations of colours, with or without text, and in negative form on a coloured ground. It can also be abstracted so that the text, or one element thereof, is removed entirely and it may still be recognized as the symbol of London's transport.

COLOUR

As long as humans have had access to precious metals, stones and materials for dyeing textiles or painting surfaces, colour has been used to indicate social, political and military relationships. The means by which the shapes and colours of symbols have been employed has varied and recurred over the centuries so that, for example, certain symbols of the Roman Empire from around the beginning of the first millennium AD were appropriated by both the German and Italian fascist movements in the early twentieth century, and the flag of the United States of America has had many manifestations and interpretations around a common theme since around 1776. Early railway-operating companies, as private organizations vying with each other for custom, adopted the military practice of using insignia and heraldic devices to identify their vehicles, premises and publicity. Every locomotive, train carriage, freight vehicle and building had to be protected from dirt and deterioration, so in their use of colour these companies were limited by the practicality of needing low-maintenance paint in enormous quantities: red, blue, green, black, or more occasionally light blue, bright green or yellow. When the cost of labour to clean vehicles increased, the colours were reviewed to ensure they would perform without regular attention. To distinguish their operations the railways used full or abbreviated company names, initials and monograms, and sometimes also the heraldic devices of cities that they served.

In the organizational hierarchy of London Transport and its predecessors, two colours stand out: red and blue. These were adopted for the Underground's bar-and-circle station nameboards in 1908, and for the bar-and-circle symbol in 1918. There is little ambiguity in distinguishing these primary hues from each other, and with white they appear distinct, assertive and reliable. Red is positively associated with strength and courage, and as the colour of life. It is eye-catching and visually arresting. Blue can represent royalty, truthfulness and hope. Red and blue are colours long associated with London, in the uniforms of its public servants and objects such as telephone kiosks and letter boxes. They are also the two most popular colours for flags in modern times, combined with white. White lettering on a blue background gives excellent legibility. Stations and other buildings were painted in the tradition of railway-company architectural styles until the 1920s, when architect Charles Holden began to specify buildings which were self-coloured and needed no additional treatment. To decorate his stations, Holden adapted the bar and circle as a sign, symbol and pattern. In this way the red and blue of the device became a frequent feature of these new, totally designed station environments.

Competing in the teeming and unregulated streets of the city, London's horse buses used bright paint colours on the bodies of their carriages to attract custom. Colour was quick and easy to recognize, and one of the obvious choices was red. London Transport painted its central and suburban buses, trolleybuses and trams red, and its country buses and Green Line coaches green. Signs to indicate road-vehicle stopping points were colour coded accordingly: red for central, suburban and country buses, including trolleybuses; green for coaches; blue for trams.

After the creation of London Transport in 1933, employees working for different parts of the organization received colour-coded insignia: blue

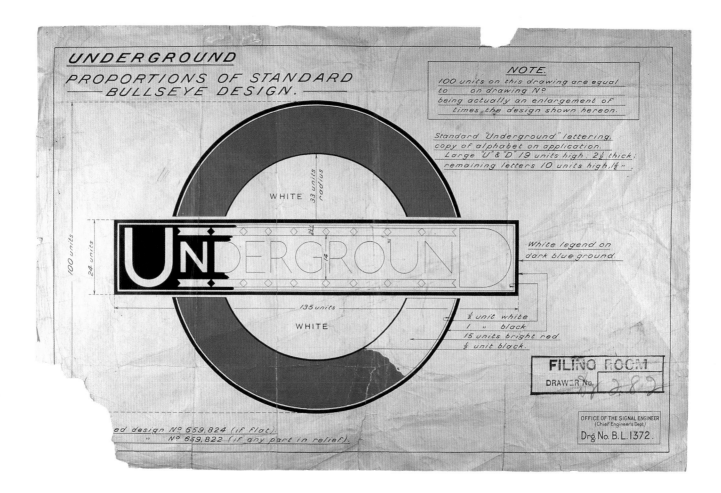

Drawing of the proportions for Edward Johnston's roundel, *c.* 1925.

for bus staff working in central London and the suburbs; yellow ochre for railway staff; red for tram and trolleybus staff, and green for country bus and Green Line coach staff. By 1908, a range of colours had been introduced to indicate the different ownership of railway lines operating through the city centre.[5] In 1933 there were six distinct colours, by 1979 nine colours, and in 2013 there are thirteen. Frank Pick tried to eliminate black from the line diagram in 1938 but found that he was unable to do so.[6] Transport for London uses additional colours to represent different transport divisions or modes. Subsequent chapters of this book will describe and illustrate many examples of how the bar and circle has been rendered in all these colours in order to give a spectrum of identities founded in a common meaning.

A LOGO FOR LONDON

Throughout its history, the bar and circle has been modern, but with a heritage; adaptable, but coherent; serious and fun. As new transport services come to London – with or without external sponsors, and below the streets or suspended from cables – so the bar-and-circle symbol continues to identify the system and is thereby reasserted as London's brand. But isn't this abstract device something else too? When it is seen in London, we know we are close to transportation services; in a global context it has become shorthand for the city itself. Rare for a device sponsored by an established organization, the logo is 'cool' too. Such is its strength as a visual symbol of the city, the bar and circle has inspired other areas of culture such as fashion and pop music, and been juxtaposed with other iconic British brands such as Fred Perry clothing. Beyond even this widespread understanding, the long association of the bar and circle with the word *Underground* has seen the symbol adopted unofficially to define ideas, activities and products as being in vogue, edgy, different. Its ability to be rapidly recognized in such contexts has seen it used on record album covers, badges, patches, posters, baseball caps and pretty much every form of memorabilia. This book features the best and the most intriguing of these adaptations and associations.

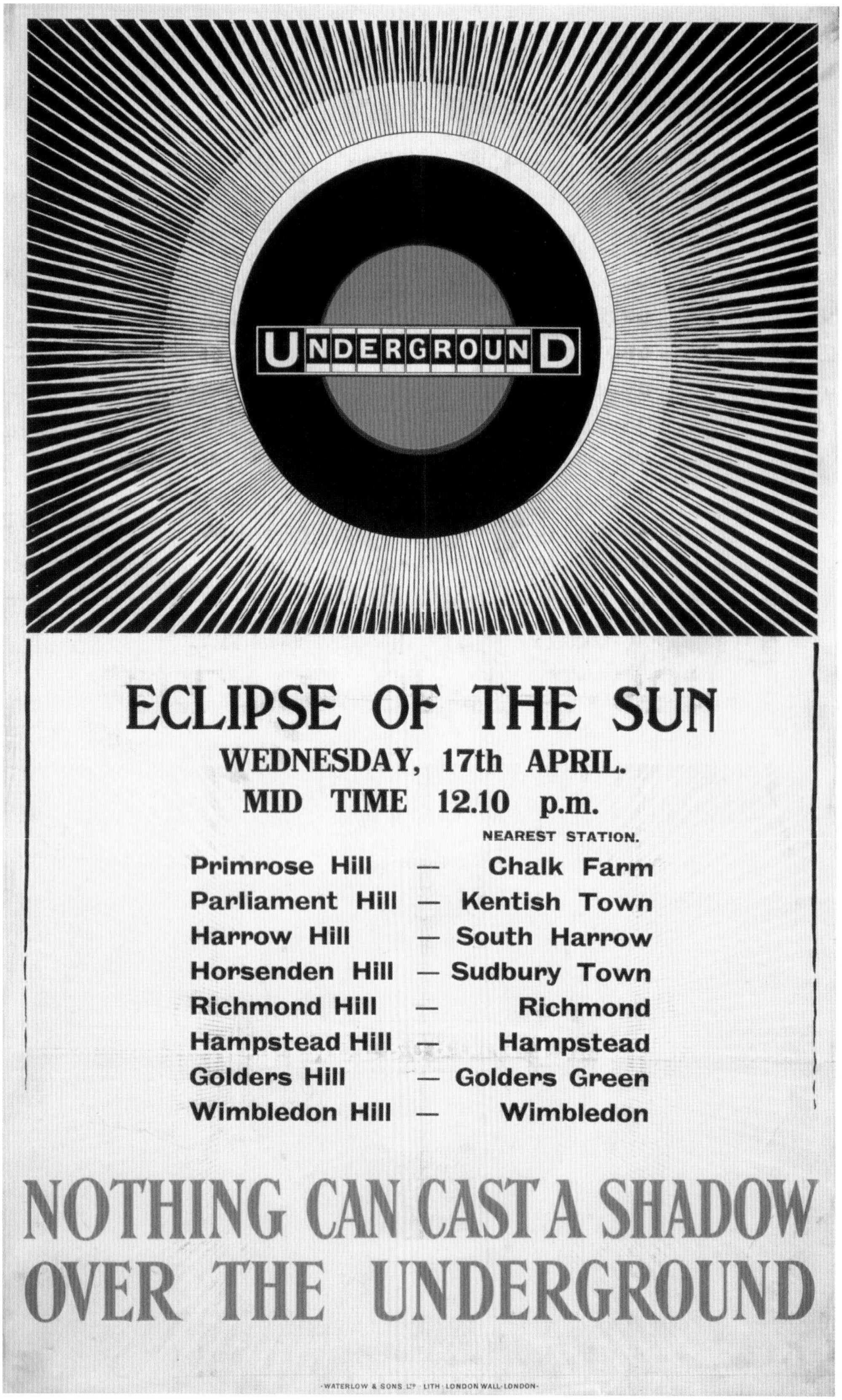

'Eclipse of the Sun', poster by Charles Sharland, 1912.

1

SELLING THE INVISIBLE
TAKE THE TUBE, BUS AND TRAM

We will never be sure what future the innovators of the bar and circle envisioned for their creation, as few contemporary records survive. When seeking to document the provenance of their symbol, the senior management of London Transport could not themselves determine accurately how it had been created, even when some of the original development team were still living to offer their memories. Any evidence is found in numerous anecdotes, retirement speeches, claims and counter-claims for the authorship of the symbol. Several individuals are central to the development of the bar and circle, working in close proximity and within a short period of time.

While we now commonly associate it with London's transport system as a complete entity, the symbol emerged from two distinct sources and transport modes: motor buses and underground railways. It evolved from separate but related needs: one to identify subterranean station platforms, and the other to indicate ownership of vehicles. Its emergence and proliferation across London was given impetus by modern American influence and Parisian design styling, and refined through classical calligraphic techniques. The application of the bar and circle did not occur in a linear fashion, nor was it consistently applied for several years. To clarify the process that culminated in the symbol we recognize today, this chapter is structured as a timeline of events.

1905

In the late nineteenth century, in crowded streets without regulation of transport services, London bus operators adopted coloured liveries and symbols to distinguish their vehicles and services from others. Established in the capital in 1855, the Anglo-French London General Omnibus Company (LGOC – or, more commonly, 'the General') was the leading operator of bus services in London at the beginning of the twentieth century.

The winged wheel logo of the London General Omnibus Company (LGOC) on a bus, photographed 1906, and a cap badge issued to bus crews 1910–14.

It made a swift transition from horse to internal combustion engine as the prime mover for its buses, and this prompted a review of the colours and symbols displayed on the General's services. A man identified only as 'Mr Crane' was closely involved with the procurement of the first motorbus chassis, and the construction of the passenger-vehicle bodies for them. Mr Crane proposed a new device to his employers: a spoked bus wheel embellished with wings after the myth of Hermes, Greek god of travellers and roads, and the messenger of the gods. Across this wheel Crane placed the name General on a bar – and so the first bar-and-circle symbol for a London transport organization was born.[1] Mr Crane had considerable foresight in his choice of design, as many railway companies internationally have since used wheels sprouting wings to identify their services. The General's winged wheel design was carried on buses from 1905 to 1912, when it was dropped in favour of the more succinct 'GENERAL' fleet name. It remained in evidence as part of the General's staff uniform until about 1918. The London Road Car Company, a rival of the General, displayed a simplified bar-and-circle design on the front of its buses from 1906.

1906

The Metropolitan District Railway, which started operating in 1868 with steam-locomotive-hauled trains over most of what is now London Underground's District line, found itself in financial difficulties at the turn of the twentieth century. In 1902, it was bought by an American-backed consortium for the purposes of electrification, and for the acquisition and development of three deep-level railways: the Baker Street and Waterloo; the Charing Cross, Euston and Hampstead; and the Great Northern, Piccadilly and Brompton. Three street-tramway companies – the Metropolitan Electric, South Metropolitan Electric and London United – operating in the western half of outer London completed the collection of networks. It was all administered by the Underground Electric Railways of London Ltd (UERL), which for ease was referred to as the Underground Group.[2] In this way, the name 'Underground' came into its now famous association with London. Because they were to be constructed in cast-iron tunnels, the deep-level projects were called 'tube' railways, and for marketing purposes their names were conveniently abbreviated to Bakerloo Tube, Hampstead Tube and Piccadilly Tube.

Architect Leslie Green (1875–1908) had the arduous task of designing 46 stations for the tubes in just four years; in poor health, the project exhausted him and he died in 1908 aged 33. Green gave considerable thought to designing the stations as confident, bright 'shopfronts' for the

Exterior of Dover Street (now Green Park) station, *c.* 1911, designed by Leslie Green as one of a series of standard Underground station buildings, and now demolished.

system, clearly part of a uniform family of buildings. Each had a ruby-red terracotta façade, with white or golden lettering moulded into the ceramic blocks. Beyond the entrances, Green aimed for the most efficient operating conditions to ease the traveller's path from street to train. The Underground Group was already exploring ways to present station names clearly in this new environment – in the absence of the usual topographical landmarks, how were travellers to recognize their stop? A press report of the Baker Street and Waterloo Railway station platforms published in the opening month of March 1906 stated that 'the general colour scheme adopted throughout the line [on the platforms] represents an innovation . . . the object of this colour system is to enable passengers to identify the stations without that anxious searching among advertising placards for the official announcement which is so difficult to find on most railways'.[3] Green specified that the name of the station form part of the tiled surface, in a limited number of positions along the platform wall. This was an advance indeed, but it was soon affected by the need to sell advertising space on the tube platforms, and the posters subsequently pasted onto the walls obscured the tiling patterns and competed with the station name panels.

The station platform at Westminster Bridge (now Westminster) station, c. 1890, showing a mass of advertisements and a rather obscured nameboard.

Communicating to the public through advertising hoardings was the most important way for businesses to sell products and services at the time, there being no television and very little use of colour in widely disseminated print media. In keeping with the general practice of mounting advertisements conspicuously, the District Railway made a substantial income from selling advertising space, and being gifted with extensive walls because its installations were largely subterranean, the temptation to smother all visible surfaces with advertising and signs could not be avoided.

Like other railway companies, the District Railway only displayed the station name two or three times along its platforms. Consequently the nameboards were hard to see. In parallel with developments for the three Tubes, the District Railway was subject to modernization as it introduced electrically powered trains. Decades of steam-train services had made the stations dirty, and in some cases structurally unsound. Like the General bus company with its brightly painted vehicles and new symbol, some visible form of improvement was necessary to enlighten rail travellers to the progress being made. This is where the other key strand of the bar-and-circle story begins.

Joseph Carter, Company Secretary for the District, decided early in 1906 'that station nameplates should be the most conspicuous part of the platform' and experimented with designs.[4] It is likely that he collaborated with the District Railway architect Harry W. Ford on the possibilities for re-signing stations. Carter 'decided that two halves of a circle would be simplest and most effective'. Independently, calligrapher Edward Johnston (1872–1944), who was to design the famous London Underground sans-serif typeface and redraw the bar-and-circle symbol, wrote in 1906 about 'the letters at Railway Stations, street corners & other places, enamelled in white on blue … Much might be done in arrangement of neighbouring signs, & in having stated places for important signs, as at stations, so that we would know where to look for them.'[5]

1907

Needing new management, the Underground Group recruited staff from north-east England and the United States. Frank Pick (1878–1941) and Walter Gott (fl. 1906–46) joined in spring 1906, and Albert Stanley (later Lord Ashfield, 1st Baron Ashfield of Southwell; 1874–1948) came from America to become General Manager in February 1907. Pick and Gott shared the task of promoting the Underground Group's activities to

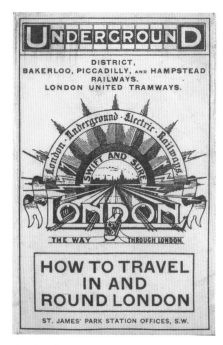

The 'Swift and Sure' motif, designed in 1907 and used to publicize the Bakerloo, Piccadilly and Hampstead Tubes. On this leaflet it is paired with the UndergrounD logotype designed by architect Harry Ford in 1908.

potential travellers. Frank Pick's endeavours and achievements in the development of design for urban transport and civil society have been celebrated for decades. He had trained as an accountant, but had a keen interest in design and was engaged in factions promoting good design in Britain. Pick had contact with many progressive industrial designers and artists, and with concepts of modernity emerging across Europe. Walter Gott is not a well-known figure, but he played a major role in the opening of the Piccadilly Tube, and when the Underground contracted out its advertising Gott was liaison agent for the contractor. He was therefore central to discussions about the public face of the Underground, and the arrangement of advertising on station platforms. He worked with the *London Evening News* in 1907 on a competition for which readers were invited to design a trading symbol for the Underground Group. The winning design, 'Swift and Sure', was used by Gott for joint publicity of the Bakerloo, Piccadilly and Hampstead Tubes.[6]

Development of the group's identity continued rapidly. Just after the last of the three Tubes opened in July 1907, the London Passenger Traffic Conference was convened by the Managing Director of the UERL, Sir George Gibb.[7] This brought together the general managers of the subterranean London railways, which included the Metropolitan Railway (operator of routes now forming parts of the Circle, Hammersmith & City and Metropolitan lines, as well as a main line north-west from London), the Underground Group (routes including parts of the Bakerloo, District, Northern and Piccadilly lines), the Central London Railway (part of the present Central line), the City & South London Railway and the Great Northern & City Railway (both now part of the Northern line). Albert Stanley achieved the brilliant move of persuading his colleagues and competitors to adopt the name of his own organization as a means of advertising a coordinated network to the public. Styled by architect Harry Ford (1875–1947), the 'UndergrounD' logotype comprised large initial and final letters in white on a blue ground, following the colour scheme typical of railway signs in Britain and overseas.[8] In the form of the logotype used for posters and publicity, there were bars or 'counters' above and below the intermediate letters to enhance the visual impact. The design would form the basis of the London Underground symbol for several decades. Albert Stanley disliked the word 'tube', and saw that all references to it on buildings and in print were replaced by the term 'Underground'. Leslie Green's stations, which were just a few years old at this time, were carefully reconstructed to feature the new trading name in blue and white on their terracotta façades.

Posters were the most important means by which the Underground and its successors communicated with the public. Colourful, humorous and informative, posters did not only induce in viewers the desire to travel, but also a sense that there was a need to visit places not previously considered. Beyond the possibility of the advertised journey, the traveller would then encounter the system directly, and see other opportunities to make use of Underground Group services – and so the effect of the initial poster viewing would continue.

During this period we return to Joseph Carter, who was now working with Albert Stanley. With the District Railway stations being cleaned and whitened – modernized and refurbished – in conjunction with electrification, the opportunity arose to address the issue of station signing. As interchange between the three tube railways would greatly increase passenger traffic, travellers had to be aided by good information and directional signs. It was all-important that every sign be made to save passengers from wasting time in finding their trains. Carter suggested to Stanley that the standard arrangement of three nameboards (with letters 2 feet [60 cm] tall) on platforms was inadequate because of the crowded trains, busy platforms and curved walls of the tunnel-station platforms, and made his experiments of 1906 known.[9] Stanley then visited the Paris Metro, where a scheme to deal with the problems of clear station signing had been introduced.[10]

1908

Throughout this period all design work on the London Underground was done in-house, with a team of railway officials convened to work on the station-sign project. Early in 1908 Frank Pick was made responsible, alongside Harry Carr (fl. 1908–46),[11] for the Underground's publicity. Working with Stanley, Carter, Pick and Carr were W.F. Blake, District Railway Superintendent of the Line; station inspector William Cleal; and Walter Gott. Christian Barman, Pick's biographer, wrote that 'Walter Gott remembered how Pick managed to convince Stanley that "fewer advertisements well spaced out and displayed in an orderly fashion would bring twice as much revenue as the old method of filling every available space with a mass of different shapes and sizes"'.[12] Signs were tested on the platforms of the station directly below the Underground's headquarters – St James's Park. Copying the Paris example, white boards 12 feet (3.6 m) high by 6 feet (1.8 m) wide were installed a railway-carriage length apart, with blue nameplates 5 feet (1.5 m) long carrying letters 6 inches (15 cm) tall. To

The bar-and-circle station nameboard was rendered in various forms across the Underground system before standard designs were prepared. For the District Railway at South Kensington, the red disc was almost the width of the blue bar, while at Boston Manor it was somewhat smaller, and more evidently a forerunner of the symbol we know today. The platform at Warwick Avenue shows how signs in tube stations were mounted at different heights to improve visibility. At Alperton, an example of one of the earliest hand-made signs was still in use in 1929.

fully distinguish the nameplates from all other advertising matter, some visual device was needed. Joseph Carter reminded the team of his 1906 sign experiment.[13] Red paper half discs were made and pasted above and below the nameplates.

After the St James's Park test signs, a Mr W. Lowe was told to mock up designs on paper to determine the appropriate proportions of circle and bar. Lowe and W.F. Blake showed Frank Pick the several paper models, and Pick selected the one he thought most suitable. Looking back in 1954, Walter Gott, who had been responsible for producing much of the Underground's printed publicity – 'illustrated leaflets, picture postcards and folder maps'[14] – claimed that his 'original design was the "genesis" of the present symbol'.[15] But there is more to the story: Gott's colleague Harry Carr 'served an exacting apprenticeship under Mr Frank Pick … His first duty in his new department was to re-arrange siting of advertisements and to put into effect the bulls-eye system of station names. And as time went on our station advertisement displays attracted world-wide interest and attention: they became models of neat-ness of layout; while the bulls-eye became a symbol of London Transport.'[16]

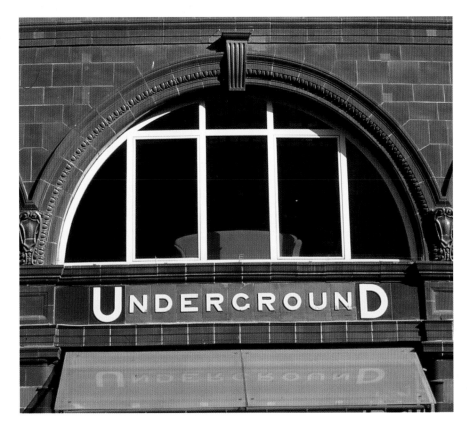

Harry Ford's UndergrounD logotype was added to station exteriors (in this instance Covent Garden) from 1908.

From autumn 1908, the bar-and-disc nameboards were installed on the District Railway and the three deep-level lines owned by the Underground Group.[17] Now the company had both the blue-bar and red-disc sign and the blue and white UndergrounD logotype at its disposal for advertising purposes. Advertising a new system to a busy city called for brevity of name. With *Underground* there was no mistaking the presence of the subterranean railway. The UndergrounD sign was installed outside stations across London, replacing the 'Swift and Sure' slogan and the official reference to 'Tubes'.

1909

Frank Pick became Traffic Officer – head of the Underground Group's new Traffic, Development and Advertising Department – in April 1909. He worked initially to improve the standard of publicity posters, but incrementally he brought significant and positive change to all aspects of the group's visual appearance. Under Pick, Walter Gott and Harry Carr, the bar and disc would emerge from the tunnels under London to announce the organization and its invisible wonders to the citizens of London. The team first applied the UndergrounD logotype to posters in 1909.

1910–11

Albert Stanley became Managing Director of the Underground Group in 1910, replacing Sir George Gibb. Now Stanley could bring his full experience of North American business and transportation practice to the context of London. With Pick as his deputy, Stanley was able to push forward the modernization and marketing of the Underground, and restructure it to gain an ever-increasing monopoly in the capital. The group's three deep-level lines were merged to become the London Electric Railway on 1 July 1910. Expanding on the concept of unification under the common trading name UndergrounD, the organization increasingly featured the logotype on its posters and other printed material, as well as outside stations. For maps showing the group's lines in the company of other operators – a very effective way of promoting the all-important interchange traffic – a special logotype labelled 'London Underground Railways' was in use from 1909 to 1912.

The London Underground Railways logo, which was commonly used in advertising material and signage between 1909 and 1912.

1912

A major advance in road and rail transport coordination came with the group's acquisition of the London General Omnibus Company in January 1912. Now the group had the General's winged wheel symbol as part of its visual identity. This asset was not lost on Pick and his team, who took the bar-and-circle arrangement of the General symbol and the bar and disc of their own station nameboards to produce the first example of its use on printed publicity in May 1912 with the leaflet 'London's Guiding Star'. Here the functional beauty of the device, and its symbolism as representative of an organization intrinsic to the city, are cleverly brought together. Charles Sharland, who was a lithographic artist at the Underground's preferred printers Waterlow & Sons, designed posters for them between 1908 and 1922. Sharland immediately took up the bar-and-disc symbol for his posters 'Eclipse of the Sun' (see p. 16) and 'Points for Whitsuntide' (both 1912), and used it in several ingenious designs. At the same time, and following Underground practice, the winged wheel was streamlined to produce a plain ring and bar showing the word 'GeneraL', and this appeared on leaflets immediately and on uniforms from 1914.[18] In the same year, the old Wood Lane Central line station was built with a parapet showing the bar and disc in coloured mosaic, and similar renderings were provided at Maida Vale and Charing Cross (now Embankment). It did not feature on vehicles. For practical purposes, the block form of the UndergrounD logotype was easier to fit into poster and publicity layouts, and was now well established with the public on station buildings. Until the mid-1930s, the logotype continued to be specified alongside other trading symbols, the bar and circle being not yet established as the single identifying mark.

Exterior of Wood Lane station, photographed in 1935, showing the bar and disc in coloured mosaic on the parapet, constructed 1914. The station building was dismantled in 2003–5 for construction of the Westfield retail centre at White City.

1913

The Underground Group continued its growth strategy, gaining control of two more important deep-level lines in 1913: the Central London Railway (part of the present Central line) and the City & South London Railway (part of the present Northern line). Coordinated publicity was ever more important. Bar-and-disc signs were added to platforms on the lines as they were rebuilt for greater capacity.

ABOVE, L–R: 'London's Guiding Star', leaflet, 1912; 'Points for Whitsuntide', poster by Charles Sharland, 1912. Both are early examples of the inventive graphical use of the bar-and-disc symbol.

RIGHT: Bar-and-ring cap badges issued to the Underground's General bus company crews 1913–33, and to crews of the Underground's three street tramway fleets 1914–33.

Albert Luxton, a driver for the London General Omnibus Company, is seen here wearing the company's insignia of a winged wheel. Luxton became a hero posthumously in 1912, when he deliberately crashed a bus, fatally injuring himself, in order to prevent it causing many more casualties as it ran down Highgate Hill in north London. The photograph of Luxton's mourners demonstrates the widespread and consistent use of the LGOC badge. The card printed to commemorate his death features one of the earliest known artistic interpretations of the bar and circle – as a wreath of flowers.

1914–18

Refining of the symbol which would become the epitome of urban London life took place deep in the countryside of southern England. Inspired by the craft teachings of William Morris, the artist and designer Eric Gill had moved to the village of Ditchling, near Hassocks, East Sussex, in 1907. The calligrapher Edward Johnston followed him in 1916. There he joined a community of people dedicated to reviving traditional craft skills on the premise that they offered timeless beauty and function, and were therefore necessary in a world where the negative effects of modernity were being seen in everyday artefacts.

While the First World War placed its own extraordinary demands on society and industry, the Underground had to keep running its transport systems. Frank Pick became influenced by 'a small group of people who were trying to reform English typography and printing design' – Harold

The first appearance of the bar-and-circle symbol in red and blue, 1918.

The YMCA bar and triangle logo, 1917.

Independent of the Underground Group and operating main-line services through the Home Counties and north-western suburbs to central London, the Metropolitan Railway introduced its own version of the new sign in 1914, distinguishing its stations by displaying a red diamond crossed by a blue bar.

Curwen, Gerard Meynell and Edward Johnston.[19] Pick was also involved in the formation of the Design & Industries Association in 1915, aimed at promoting good design after the example of the Deutscher Werkbund.[20] The following year Pick announced his intentions to reform lettering across the Underground, including the very important station name-boards. In his vision for a new fount, Pick cited Eric Gill's painted lettering for a W.H. Smith shop fascia in Paris, saying 'each letter must be a strong and unmistakeable symbol with a high degree of individuality; it must have the greatest possible carrying power, with the character of an official railway sign that was not to be mistaken by people in a hurry for a trader's advertisement'.[21] To realize his vision, Frank Pick commissioned Edward Johnston to design a typeface exclusively for Underground Group use; the first drafts of what Johnston called the railway 'block letter alphabet' were made in late 1915, and preliminary designs were submitted in mid-1916.[22] This became the standard typeface for all communications between the Underground Group and its public, both printed formally in woodblock letterpress, and hand-drawn for lithographic printing. Building on the relationship developed during the design of the Underground typeface, at the turn of 1916/17 Pick asked Johnston to review the trading marks used by the group. They had the General's bar-and-circle symbol to hand, and the bar and disc of the station nameboards which had begun to feature on posters combined with the UndergrounD logotype. During the war the YMCA/YWCA was engaged in relief work, providing refreshments and other support. Pick had seen their logo of an open triangle crossed by a bar. He suggested that Johnston produce 'something like it "but more balanced"', sketching ideas for an UndergrounD symbol characterized by a ring instead of a disc.[23]

While Johnston worked on the task, Pick had the various printers used by the Underground make up approximations of the mark. Red was introduced for the ring, and blue for the bar. Equipped with a goose quill in his quest to revive and celebrate the art of calligraphy,[24] Edward Johnston, single-handedly and by hundredths of an inch, married classical lettering with modernity. For the Underground, he ruthlessly discarded the florid typography and gilded heraldry that Victorian engineering had taken up to assert its heritage. The rigour which Johnston had brought to the typeface design process, and which would also contribute to the bar-and-circle symbol's adaptability and longevity, is evident in Johnston's thought 'that Pick was too much concerned with appearances, with what would *look* well'.[25] Johnston himself approached the problem with 'the austerity of an engineer'.[26] Johnston presented Pick with an UndergrounD

UNDERGROUND

Edward Johnston's first 'UndergrounD' label or logotype, designed 1916 (reconstructed by Justin Howes, *c.* 1990).

'label' in 1916, soon after the typeface design and evidently derived from it. Streamlined and succinct, it took advantage of the curved letter forms in Johnston's own railway block letters, and it was an attempt to devise a brand mark which would work well on posters. It would form the basis for the marking of railway carriages for several decades, but the lightness of the typeface made it visually weak for a symbol representative of the organization.

This logotype was superseded in mid-1917 by a label in which the word UndergrounD was reversed out of a coloured background, and the intermediate letters bordered above and below by 'ribbons' pierced with the lozenge points or stops of Johnston's typeface. The ribbons continued the Underground practice of using hyphens to balance the smaller letters with the larger capitals of the 1908 logotype. Now, Johnston used the ribbons to reduce the areas of solid colour across the label, and so give it further legibility and visual impact.

1919–20

A trial version of the new Underground symbol appeared in spring 1917, but it was not used widely until late 1919.[27] In the final version Johnston subtly but definitively altered the proportions of all parts of the symbol. The letters were redrawn to a bolder weight, reducing the black area and condensing the U and D. The bar was fractionally larger than before; the ring was of the same diameter, but thinner, so increasing the area of the white centre. Pick gave a free hand to artists invited to design publicity posters: their production was one area where he felt the work was more important than a rigid application of a corporate style. The output of consistently innovative posters made its own style for the organization. Frequently no symbol featured on the posters at all, with perhaps just the word 'Underground' reproduced in hand-drawn lettering. Often the UndergrounD logotype was more convenient for the design, being of plain horizontal shape like other text and taking up less space. However, artists such as Henry C. Beck, F.C. Herrick, Arnrid Johnston, Alan Rogers

Edward Johnston's bulls-eye. Two styles of the symbol, with different proportions, were used until 1933.

DO NOT ATTEMPT TO ENTER A CROWDED CAR

Trains are delayed by Passengers trying to force their way into a full train. The more trains, the more seats. The shorter the stop at the station, the more trains.

Train delays mean overcrowding

The first use of the Johnston logotype with plain ring on a poster is on George Morrow's 'Do not attempt to enter a crowded car', 1918.

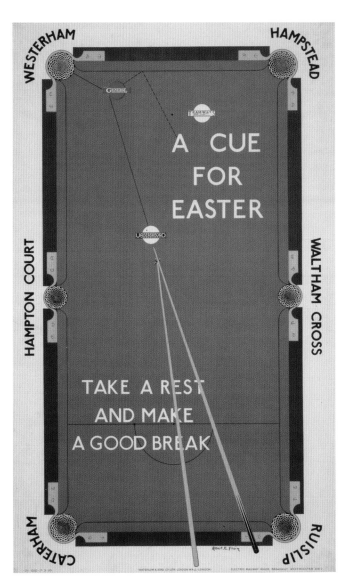

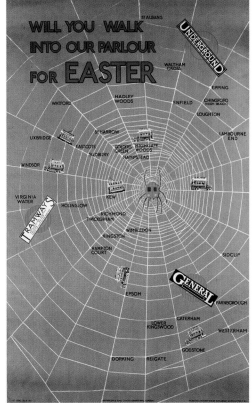

Before Johnston had completed his logotype designs for the London Underground, the organization had a mixed set of bar-and-circle symbols, as seen here on the poster 'Will you walk into our parlour for Easter', by Charles Sharland, 1920 (ABOVE). The same symbols were reinterpreted for the poster 'A cue for Easter', by Albert E. Fruin, also 1920 (LEFT).

and Charles Sharland did grasp the pictorial possibilities of the bar and disc and bar and circle, devising ingenious and witty versions which emphasized the centrality of the Underground to London life, for business and pleasure.

At the beginning of the 1920s, the bar and circle was established as a symbol by which to recognize transport services in the city, and as a family of logotypes to identify each component of the transport network. The next phase of development in this visual identity would see further advances in the use of the symbol as it was adapted and evolved by the expanding organization.

THIS WEEK
IN LONDON

Monday, 5th December   to   Saturday, 10th December

LECTURES

"THE TOWER IN NORMAN TIMES"   Tower of London
Tuesday 11 a.m.   Mark Lane Station
"ROMAN LONDON" (MONDAY 2.30 p.m.) "SAXON LONDON" (FRIDAY 2.30 p.m.)
London Museum, St. James, S.W.   Dover Street Station
ANCIENT EUROPEAN HISTORY   (WEEKDAYS at 12 noon & 3 p.m.)
British Museum   Holborn or British Museum Stn.
"BUSINESS, PLEASURE & ART"   Victoria & Albert Museum
Thursday 5-6 p.m.   South Kensington Station

CONCERTS

B.B.C. SYMPHONY CONCERT   Queens Hall, Langham Place
Wednesday, 8.15 p.m.   Oxford Circus Station
JOHN McCORMACK (In aid of Safer Motherhood)   Royal Albert Hall
Thursday, 8 p.m.   South Kensington Station
POPULAR CONCERT   Central Hall, Westminster
Saturday, 7.30 p.m.   Westminster or St. James Pk. Stn.
HANDEL'S "MESSIAH" (KINGSWAY HALL CHORAL SOCIETY)   Kingsway Hall
Saturday, 7.30 p.m.   Holborn Station
ADELA VERNE, SCHUMANN - BRAHMS RECITAL
Wigmore Hall, Wigmore Street
Saturday, 3 p.m.   Oxford Circus or Bond St. Stn.

DOG RACING

CATFORD STADIUM   Tues., Fri. & Sat., 8 p.m.
    Victoria, Strand or Cannon St. Stn. (thence Southern Rly)
CLAPTON STADIUM   Tues. & Thurs. 8 p.m. (SATURDAY 3.15 & 8 p.m.)
    Finsbury Park Station (thence bus)
HARRINGAY STADIUM   Mon., Wed. & Fri., 8 p.m.
    Manor House Station
WEMBLEY STADIUM   Mon., Wed. & Sat. 8 p.m.
    Wembley Station
WEST HAM STADIUM   Mon. & Wed. 8 p.m. (SATURDAY 3.15 & 8 p.m.)
    Plaistow Station (thence tram)
WHITE CITY STADIUM   Tues., Thurs. & Sat. 8 p.m.
    Wood Lane Station
WIMBLEDON STADIUM   Wed., Fri. & Sat. 8 p.m.
    Tooting Broadway Station

(For Ice Hockey, Boxing, Football and Rugby see separate poster)

BECK·32.

'This week in London', poster
by Harry Beck, 1932.

2

UNIQUELY DESIGNED
FOR LONDON

This chapter covers the period 1921 to 1939, from the point at which the Underground Group – an enterprise competing for transport business in the capital – had established its first set of trading marks, through to the commencement of the Second World War. The most significant event within the period occurred in July 1933, when the Underground Group was reconstituted as the London Passenger Transport Board (LPTB). The LPTB traded as 'London Transport' and operated a near-monopoly of rail and road services in greater London, alongside those rail routes provided by the main-line companies. There were innovations in the Underground's corporate identity throughout the 1920s, and further considerable developments in brand identity brought about by London Transport.

The chapter is in two parts. First we look at the period 1921–34 and the context of innovation in industrial design, both generally and for the Underground and London Transport specifically. The evolution of the bar-and-circle symbol is given as a verbatim dialogue between the client – the Underground Group and London Transport – and the designer – Edward Johnston. After this section of correspondence, individual applications of the symbol are discussed in a hierarchy of uses, across the various transport modes and from architecture to publicity and staff uniforms. In the second part we review developments in the five years 1935–9, when radical changes were made to the design and use of the London Transport brand as it set out further ambitious growth plans, cut short by the start of the Second World War.

DESIGN AFTER THE FIRST WORLD WAR

The end of the First World War in 1918 had given renewed freedom for developments in the design of printed materials. Posters, in particular, were becoming an important means by which manufacturers and retailers addressed the public. Increased sea and air travel, better communications and the use of photography meant that designers and design patrons were much more aware of developments beyond their own spheres. By the mid-1920s, one of the most influential twentieth-century design schools – the Bauhaus – would be known worldwide for its creativity in craft, design and architecture. This was a time of émigrés taking design theory and practice to all parts of Europe and the New World, promoting an apparently singular idea of modernity. The Design & Industries Association (DIA) in England had been inspired by the Deutscher Werkbund; the Underground's Frank Pick would become its president in 1930. When the government formed the Council for Art and Industry in 1934, Pick was made Chairman.

Britain had its own master craftspeople and artists. Important illustrators such as Edward Bawden, Eric Ravilious, Tom Eckersley and Dora M. Batty left art school in the 1920s and would reinvigorate British visual culture. Many progressive design companies and agencies became prominent at this time, such as Heal's in London, Dryad in Leicester, E.K. Cole Radio (EKCO), HMV electrical equipment, ISOKON, PEL furniture and the Poole Pottery (Carter, Stabler and Adams). Eric Gill produced his sans-serif typeface for the Monotype Corporation in 1926–8. This was derived from Johnston's typeface for the Underground Group, and was used by the London and North Eastern Railway to unify its publicity and signage. 'Gill sans' became an extremely popular typeface throughout the 1930s, and has enjoyed a revival in recent years as part of the British austerity-chic trend.

Industrial Design Partnership, the first formal pairing of Milner Gray and Misha Black, was founded in 1935. In their later constitution as Design Research Unit, they would be tasked with reviewing the public face of London Transport in the 1960s and 1970s (see Chapter 5). Founded by Allen Lane, the Penguin publishing imprint also commenced in 1935 and revolutionized paperback book design. There was a marked rise in the role of commercial art – what we currently know as graphic or communication design – as commercial organizations became aware of the value of effective and attractive advertising. Important patrons for UK artists in the 1920s included Shell Oil; British Petroleum (BP); the General Post Office; Imperial Chemical Industries (ICI); the high-street banks; operators of railway, road and air transport; utility companies; cigarette and drinks manufacturers; and several government ministries.

For the Underground companies, the period 1921–39 was one of extensions, additions and alterations to the railway network. Major parts of what now comprise the Bakerloo, Central, District, Northern and Piccadilly lines were under Underground control, and its only rival for rail transport across London was the Metropolitan Railway. To restart development after the First World War, the Trade Facilities Act came into force in 1921. This enabled the Underground to recommence extension plans drafted before 1914. A five-year New Works Programme was launched by the Underground in 1930. In 1933, the Underground Group became the major component of the new London Passenger Transport Board, which traded as 'London Transport'. Albert Stanley – now ennobled as Lord Ashfield – chaired the board, and Frank Pick was its Vice-chairman and Managing Director. A second substantial growth plan was announced in 1935 as the London Transport New Works Programme 1935/40. Harry Carr continued as the Underground and London Transport Assistant Publicity Manager, and in 1935 began to work for the new Publicity Officer, Christian Barman (1898–1980), an architect, industrial designer and journalist. Also working for the Underground were in-house draftspeople, including Fred Stingemore, who drew railway-line diagrams, bus and tram system maps and some posters, and H.C. (Henry) Beck, designer of the London Underground Diagram of Lines, created in 1931–3.[1]

A HIERARCHY OF USES

To understand how the bar-and-circle symbol became a core part of London's transport activities between 1921 and 1939, a summary of its various applications is helpful. Guided by the keen economic and design sense of Albert Stanley and Frank Pick, the bar and circle proliferated to become one of the first modern brands. Primarily, it was the means of indicating places to find transport services. Locations included station exteriors, road-service-vehicle stopping places and related premises such as vehicle garages and depots. The Underground bar-and-circle sign appeared outside stations from 1921.

On the Underground's railway system, we have seen how the original development of the bar and disc came from the innovation of effective display for station names. The bar and circle, too, was taken up for station nameboards from 1923. As a partner in the practice Adams, Holden and Pearson, the architect Charles Holden (1875–1960) had begun to work for the Underground in 1916, commissioned by Frank Pick. Holden exercised careful control over the design of the organization's 'shop windows' – its stations – and ensured that the buildings were good backdrops for the display of publicity. He made limited but effective use of the bar and circle as functional decoration.

Many posters of the early 1920s were simply pictorial, encouraging people to shop or travel without reference to the transport organization. BELOW, L–R: 'Shop between 10 and 4', poster by Edward McKnight Kauffer, and 'Hampton Court', poster by Charles Paine, both 1921.

For bus services provided by the London General Omnibus Company as a subsidiary of the Underground Group, the ring-and-bar symbol had started as a vehicle identifier, transferred to uniform insignia, and was then redesigned for publicity – posters and maps – and staff clothing. Towards the end of the 1910s, the first experiments were made with fixing signs along the street to show bus stopping places, and these featured variants on the bar and circle. Staff of the three Underground tramway companies wore cap badges based on the bar and circle. From 1934, a concerted effort was made to promote the organization through the bar and circle, and it became the means of identification for all uniformed staff across the different transport modes.

A high-profile manifestation of the symbol was that used for publicity posters, leaflets and system maps promoting rail and road services. In most cases, the aim was to make the public aware of some opportunity to buy goods or services, but there soon came the possibility of enriching the selling motive with well-made images to give visual pleasure. For entreaties to travel, the Underground and London Transport excelled at combining good art and design with a clear commercial message. Colour lithography had been widely used for poster reproduction since the mid-nineteenth century, although letterpress printing was still used for maps and diagrams. Lithography was very suitable for accurate renderings of artworks and the delicate mixing of colours and forms, but it was less appropriate for reproducing precise calligraphic motifs or symbols. If required on a poster, these would need to be added by a second process requiring different machines and skills, so it made economic sense for the artist to incorporate any text into their work. Harold Hutchison, London Transport Publicity Officer 1947–66, said that 'infinite pains were taken that the invitations [posters] were both arresting and tempting with a colourful challenge which was never braked by information better given inside [the station]'.[2] He added that posters should be 'works of art framed as mural decorations proportionate to the whole [station] façade. The famous bar-and-circle device is London Transport's symbol, but it is always used as an integral contribution to the elevation'.[3] This explains clearly why posters did not need to show the bar and circle; some featured other identifying marks and some did not mention the operator's name at all. Alongside the pictorial posters, free paper maps and diagrams were issued to travellers, indicating the different transport modes or networks. These were more sober affairs, models of clear information design. All system maps were identified by a distinct symbol, and through the 1920s these were taken from the growing family of bar-and-circle devices drawn by Edward Johnston.

The most important relationship for the development of the symbol during the period 1921–34 was that between Frank Pick, Harry Carr and Edward Johnston. Throughout the 1920s, Edward Johnston was retained by the Underground Group, and then London Transport, as a consultant. Harry Carr has been ignored in most histories of the Underground, but deserves credit for being a key figure who worked as the link between Frank Pick and the designers and artists he commissioned. Frank Pick knew the printer Gerard Meynell of the Westminster Press through his contacts in the Arts and Crafts movement.[4] Once Meynell had brought Pick and Johnston together to secure a commission, it was Carr who

The first three standardized symbols of the Underground Group's services – General buses, three Tramways networks and the Underground railway system – can be seen on the poster 'The countryside for Easter', by Gladys Mary Rees, 1921.

corresponded frequently with the calligrapher on the design of the first bar-and-circle symbols, and who coordinated the development process between Waterlow & Sons – the printers who produced the proof artworks – and Johnston. After Carr relinquished his post to Christian Barman, he still handled much of the day-to-day decision making in the department. In 1938, Harry Carr would report comprehensively on the use of the bar and circle across the Underground railway network.

THE CARR–JOHNSTON CORRESPONDENCE

The initial moves towards a family of trading marks got underway in the 1920s, with Edward Johnston preparing first logotypes or labels, and then bar-and-circle symbols for the various Underground Group transport networks, General buses and the combined Metropolitan, London United and South Metropolitan tramways.

A wonderful insight may be gleaned by following the dialogue between Harry Carr at the Underground Group/London Transport and Edward Johnston, through the period of transition from Underground to London Transport. Its communiqués, reports and observations bring us right into the creative context from which the classic form of the bar and circle sprang. The artworks were hand drawn by the group's official printers, Waterlow & Sons, and then photographic copies or 'pulls' (trial prints) of the artworks were sent to Edward Johnston in Ditchling, Sussex, for redrafting and adjustment. The work was slow and meticulous, and was often delivered to the Underground Group by the last post, last train or late altogether owing to the designer's insistence of arriving at the very best solution.

The organization expanded substantially at the beginning of the 1930s. It spread geographically, and it embraced new technology. Green Line long-distance express coach services across London, from key outlying towns at a radius of about 30 miles (roughly 50 km) from Charing Cross, started operation in summer 1930 under the control of the Underground's General subsidiary. The network was rapidly augmented over the following year. Trolleybuses – electric vehicles taking power from overhead cables – began to operate in south-west London in place of trams on 16 May 1931. The General was now running bus routes out into the rural land around London, linking villages and nascent suburbs with interchange points for onward travel.[5] As the group developed its businesses, marketing of the new services brought passengers and prestige. Johnston was called upon to produce new versions of the ring and bar, which he began calling a 'bulls-eye'; this is the term we will use from this point forwards. We join the Carr–Johnston conversation in March 1931, when Harry Carr commissioned additions to the family of service identifiers.

> 20 March 1931. Dear Mr. Johnston, We are wanting a block [logotype] for our Green Line services similar to the "General" block … We should also like blocks reading: Green LinE CoachwayS, GeneraL BuswayS, UndergrounD RailwayS. Would it be too much to ask you to sketch these out for us also? We hardly like to say that we should like the blocks as soon as possible as we are desirous of including these in our posters.[6]

These proposals – with their 'Coachways' and 'Busways' appellations – are interesting because they reflect the influence of Lord Ashfield in Americanizing the London system. The slogan 'Another General Busway' had been used on posters in 1930. Underground Railways was a name used in publicity from 1908.

> 21 April 1931. Dear Mr. Carr, Thank You for your note of 20th. I have made some preliminary experiments, but a difficulty (the U-D treatment of Two words) turns out greater than I had foreseen. "Green Lines", it seems to me, can hardly be satisfactorily treated thus, GreeN LineS, but could be made thus, Green LineS, or thus, GreeN LineS.[7]

> 22 April 1931. Dear Mr. Johnston, as requested, we are sending herewith pulls of the various designs you have done for us, also some designs where the two line arrangement has been used, *and would point out that the Chairman is very anxious that in the new design, the bulls-eye or circle arrangement, should be incorporated* [author's italics].[8]

Johnston designed a Green Line symbol within a few weeks, but the Underground Group could not decide whether to stay with this or pursue the more transatlantic style of branding:

> 30 April 1931. Dear Mr. Johnston, Thank you very much for the drawing of the Green Line block. We will let you know our decision in regard to it in the course of a few days time. With regard to the block for the Green Line Coachways, we should like to have two drawings – one in one line and one in two lines as you suggest, as some of our publications will carry the two-line block better than one long one.[9]

The poster 'Passingford Bridge', by Clive Gardiner, 1930, carries the short-lived slogan 'General Busway'.

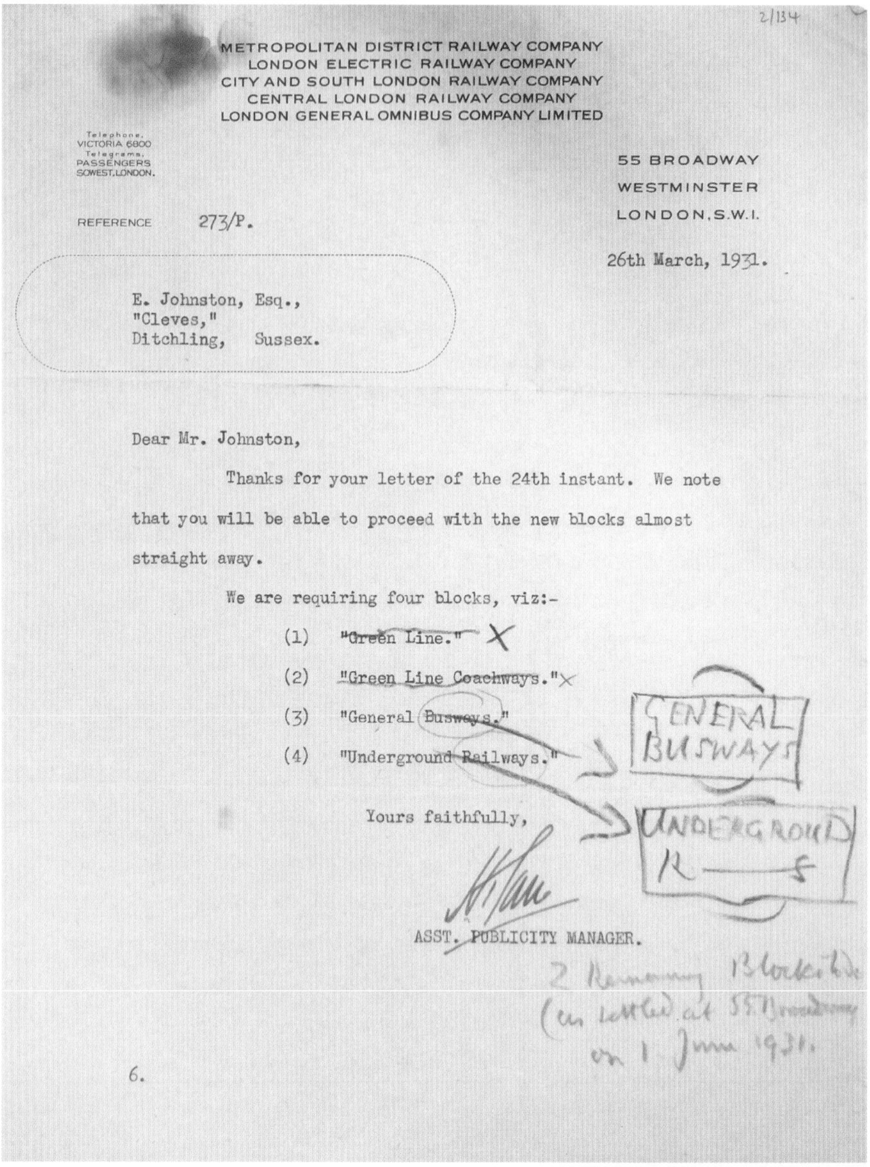

METROPOLITAN DISTRICT RAILWAY COMPANY
LONDON ELECTRIC RAILWAY COMPANY
CITY AND SOUTH LONDON RAILWAY COMPANY
CENTRAL LONDON RAILWAY COMPANY
LONDON GENERAL OMNIBUS COMPANY LIMITED

Telephone.
VICTORIA 6800
Telegrams.
PASSENGERS
SOWEST,LONDON.

55 BROADWAY
WESTMINSTER
LONDON, S.W.I.

REFERENCE   273/P.

26th March, 1931.

E. Johnston, Esq.,
"Cleves,"
Ditchling, Sussex.

Dear Mr. Johnston,

Thanks for your letter of the 24th instant. We note
that you will be able to proceed with the new blocks almost
straight away.

We are requiring four blocks, viz:-

(1)   "Green Line."

(2)   "Green Line Coachways."

(3)   "General Busways."

(4)   "Underground Railways."

Yours faithfully,

ASST. PUBLICITY MANAGER.

6.

Johnston's sketches of General Busways and Underground Railways logos (RIGHT) and Green Line Coachways logos (OPPOSITE).

These blocks posed a real challenge for Johnston because he could not satisfactorily accommodate two lines of text on a symbol with good visual proportions. The conversation went quiet for almost a year until prompted by another new Underground Group service – the electric trolleybuses, which were replacing tram services in west London from May 1931:

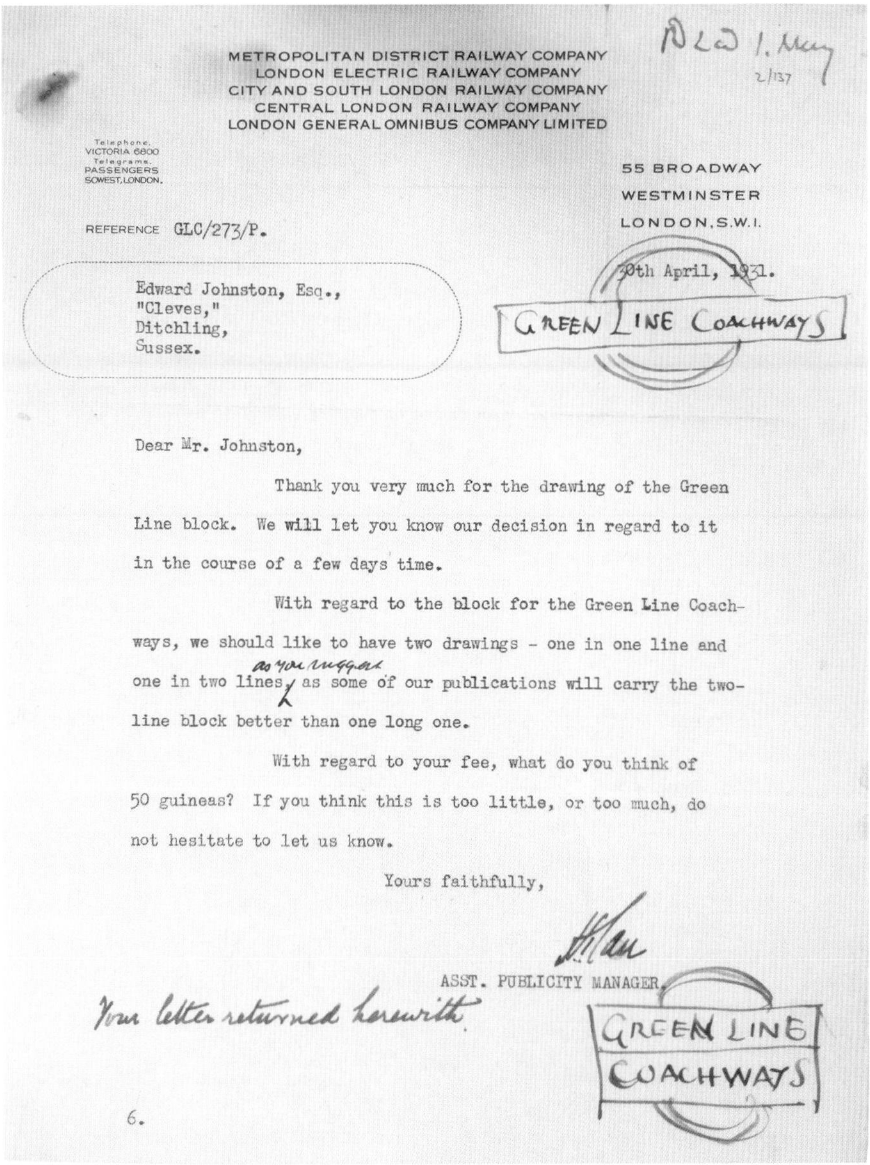

METROPOLITAN DISTRICT RAILWAY COMPANY
LONDON ELECTRIC RAILWAY COMPANY
CITY AND SOUTH LONDON RAILWAY COMPANY
CENTRAL LONDON RAILWAY COMPANY
LONDON GENERAL OMNIBUS COMPANY LIMITED

Dld 1. May 2/137

Telephone.
VICTORIA 6800
Telegrams,
PASSENGERS
SOWEST,LONDON.

55 BROADWAY
WESTMINSTER
LONDON,S.W.I.

REFERENCE GLC/273/P.

Edward Johnston, Esq.,
"Cleves,"
Ditchling,
Sussex.

30th April, 1931.

GREEN LINE COACHWAYS

Dear Mr. Johnston,

　　　　Thank you very much for the drawing of the Green Line block. We will let you know our decision in regard to it in the course of a few days time.

　　　　With regard to the block for the Green Line Coachways, we should like to have two drawings - one in one line and one in two lines, *as you suggest* as some of our publications will carry the two-line block better than one long one.

　　　　With regard to your fee, what do you think of 50 guineas? If you think this is too little, or too much, do not hesitate to let us know.

　　　　Yours faithfully,

ASST. PUBLICITY MANAGER.

Your letter returned herewith.

GREEN LINE COACHWAYS

6.

19 April 1932. Dear Mr. Johnston, Once again I am worrying you; this time for a block "TrolleybuseS" in one word, something after the style of the attached. This is urgent, and I should be obliged if you would let us have it along as soon as possible. We have not yet seen the "[General] Busways" and "Tramways" designs, but if it will not inconvenience you I should like to cancel the instruction for these, as we are not now proposing to make use of the idea.[10]

THIS WEEK
IN LONDON

'This week in London', poster by J.Z. Atkinson, 1933, carrying C.W. Bacon's 'LPTB' symbol, and the bulls-eye as the man's face.

The reference to Tramways was a mistake, because the design requested in March 1931 had been for "Underground Railways". The Underground were putting pressure on Johnston to work rather more quickly than usual:

20 April 1932. Dear Mr. Carr, Thank you for your letter of the 19th. I am quite pleased to be "worried" in this way, and am hopeful that I can let you have the block "TrolleybuseS" pretty soon. (If I can get started on it this week – which seems possible – you shall have it next week). As to the two [Busways and Tramways] labels or blocks … thankfully neglected by me – if they are no longer required, I am quite agreeable to their cancellation.[11]

22 June 1932. Dear Mr. Johnston, Thank you for sending along the trolleybus design. We have not yet come to a decision on the use of this. We have already asked you to cancel the General and Underground designs, so with the two Green Line and the one trolleybus design we propose closing the order, and take it that you will agree.[12]

It is likely that the cancellation of further blocks at this time was informed by the forthcoming organizational change, with the Underground Group becoming the London Passenger Transport Board (LPTB) in July 1933. The new ownership of the rail and road networks by an administrative body which would, for the first time in London, operate almost all public transport services prompted a review of the trading symbols. At this time, the task of 'branding' an organization was still a new area of design. The concept of giving personality to a business was experimental too. Nevertheless, how could this unified, yet invisible entity be coherently branded? Although there was now an overall trading name, should there be one identity for every part of London Transport, or a series of subsidiary identities for each service mode? Further requests were forwarded to Edward Johnston, and a commission given to commercial artist and Underground poster designer C.W. Bacon in the months running up to the Board's creation.

Both designers were briefed to consider how the initials of the Board – L P T B – could be incorporated into a symbol. Bacon drafted a winged motif, which was used on one or two booklets and posters for a few months in 1933. The symbol was *moderne* and in keeping with the fashion of the period, but it lacked colour. It was brisk and anonymous, too fragmented for an organization that wished the public to regard it as a capable and legible system.

Edward Johnston was tasked with incorporating the letters into the existing bulls-eyes. Commissioned in April 1933 and delivered five weeks later, his report – he was too busy at this time to actually redraw the designs himself – considered the fleet names General, Green Line, Underground, Tramways, Trolleybus and General Country Services.[13] In preparing his comments, Johnston made experiments with the General and Green Line bulls-eyes, considering them representative of the smaller and larger ringed versions of all the designs and therefore a model from which the others could be adapted:

Report on experiments by E.J.: The problem being to add the letters L.P.T.B. to the "Bulls-eye" Designs (while retaining the familiar features of the latter).

Notes on Outer (and Inner) LINES of Rings

The original outline 'Bulls-eye' or Ring crossed (and as it were, held together) by the Nameplate [logotype] is a perfectly sound device, but when one tries to superimpose extra elements – the several letters L.P.T.B – either within the Ring or upon its main band, these elements react on the Ring and give it an appearance of a kind of asymmetry. To put it more picturesquely, make the inner edge of the main band look raw and unfinished. To remedy this I added inner lines to all the Rings, in harmony with their outer lines.[14]

Notes on the grouping of the letters L, P, T, B.

I adopted Mr Duncan's suggestion of placing the letters L.P.T.B. inside the bulls-eye rings, and have tried also the experiment of superimposing the letters upon the rings themselves … In each case I grouped these four letters with great care to give what appeared to me the most compact, and also the best, appearance. I tried, in the case of the letters upon the main band, radiating them, i.e. making their stems point to the centre of the circle, as in a coin, but I did not find the appearance of these satisfactory unless the letters were made so large as to span the width of the main band, when they seemed to me to compete unduly with the name on the 'nameplate' – which after all, is what the public will want to see … Of the two varieties, that in which the letters are placed within the ring, seems to me clearest and best.

The LPTB version of the Underground bulls-eye. Edward Johnston added a thick line to the inside edge of the ring to visually counterbalance the extra 'weight' of the letters in the upper semicircle.

CORRIGENDUM　(by Edward Johnston 24th October, 1933).

to my Report of 23rd October on London Transport Label.

Specimen "pull" 18^{1}/16th inches long.

and on my Re-arrangement of this label - (4½% longer).

In the above Report (p.2) I said "the general reduction of the inter-letter spacing is I think justified on the ground of the total length........."

Since them I have been mentally debating that particular point and have come to the conclusion that a slight increase in the inter-letter spacing of certain adjacent letters is desirable.

I suggest therefore the following correction of my "Re-arrangement":-

```
    (Increase the present inter-letter spaces (each) by)
    (1/32nd. inch between                                )
    (       O - N,  N - D,  D - O, O - N, N - T,         )
    (       S - P,  O - R.                               )
```

+ (That is the addition of ^{1}/32nd. inch to the
  (present spaces between each of the letters in
  (ONDON -　　　　　　　　　　　A total of :　^{4}/32nd. inch

+ (The same addition to space of
  (Gap　(N - T)　　　　　　　　　"　"　"　^{1}/32nd. inch

+ (The same additional space (in
  (the word TRANSPORT) between
  (S - P and O - R, only　　　"　"　"　^{2}/32nd. inch

A grand total addition of:-　　^{7}/32nd. inch

This would make the length of my "re-arranged" label (at present about 18^{9}/10th inches) about $19\frac{3}{8}$ inches.　That is an increase in length over the original Waterlow "pull" of just under 6%.

This addition of ^{1}/32nd. inch to 7 of the inter-letter space widths seems very small, but it would have a definite effect to the good of the label (which would be still perceptible in the smallest

RIGHT AND OPPOSITE: Part of Edward Johnston's 1933 report on the London Transport bulls-eye symbol, in which the alterations needed to ensure the best proportions for the design are discussed in precise detail.

- - -
A little _less_ space
between
T & R, R & A, P & O,
would improve the
spacing.

(TR about $1/100$th inch _less_ space between these
(
(RA put these as near together as the tail of R and
(the left leg of A will go _without absolutely_
(_touching._
(
(PO about $1/100$th inch _less_ space between these

x x x x
Make a little _more_
space between N & S,
and R & T

(NS about $1/100$th inch _more_ space between these
(
(RT about $3/100$ths of an inch _more_ space between these

(These changes (in Fig. 2) should leave the _total length_ of the
word 'TRANSPORT' about _the same as it is at present_ (or perhaps
$1/100$th inch shorter) but the word 'TRANSPORT' will, I think, be
better spaced).

2.   The surcharging of the words on the bullseye design.

The _placing of the words_

CRITICISM   The plan adopted in the Waterlow 'pulls' practically
gets over the difficulty of dealing with a short word (LONDON) and
a long word (TRANSPORT) by optically "attaching" both words to the
'label'.

But this optical 'attachment' damages both the design of the
bullseye and the legibility of the words.   The bullseye loses its
clean cut structural effect by having this blurred central mass of
lettering-plus-label.   At the best it becomes a _fringed_ label
(reminding me a little of a hairy caterpillar). And this optical
'blurr' also damages the legibility and, one might say, it deprives
the words 'LONDON TRANSPORT' of their proper _force._

SUGGESTION.   There are two ways in which this might be remedied
remedied.   Both ways seem to me to give sufficiently satisfactory
results.

There were two versions of the London Transport form of the logo, before and after adjustment by Johnston.

Note on the points or 'dots' between the letters

These have also been carefully arranged and treated to get the (to me) best effect possible. I tried them in various proportions. I also tried them, on the main bands, with all 4 sides of the lozenge outlined white and they at once became of undue importance. If on the other hand the white outline was made narrower the black did not show up sufficiently but appeared to be out of focus.[15]

Johnston's adaptations were short-lived. The full trading name of 'London Transport' seemed to state exactly the purpose of the board, and Harry Carr asked Edward Johnston to design a new block logotype:

5 October 1933. Dear Mr. Johnston, It has been decided to discontinue the use of the letters "L.P.T.B." and to use "London Transport" in place thereof. As this matter was urgent we asked the artist at Waterlow's to draw up a new block for us and we are enclosing herewith pulls of all that we have had made. It occurs to us that there are one or two subtle points in your design which the artist may have overlooked and we shall be glad if you will examine them and let us have your criticisms.[16]

5 October 1933. Dear Mr. Carr, There certainly are, as you suggest, some subtle points which might be dealt with beneficially. It is very difficult with such things to find the right solution, except by a process of guess and trial. But I have not time at present for carrying that out properly by experimental drawings (nor do I suppose you could spare the time I should take!). I propose then to make a report on the designs suggesting, as specifically as possible, what alterations might be tried with a view to getting the best effects (with each design).[17]

With further consideration, Johnston added:

8 October 1933. Dear Mr. Carr, May I congratulate you and all concerned on the dropping of the name "L.P.T.B." and the substitution of London Transport. It is a typical example of English good sense. Comparable with the getting rid of nearly all the unnecessary inflexions in our grammar, while most of the other languages are still burdened with them.[18]

As usual Johnston worked out the London Transport symbol in minute detail, varying the spacing of letters by hundredths of an inch to get the optimum visual impression. The letters were all hand drawn by the technicians at the printers, according to Johnston's instructions. Once the logotype had been produced, it was incorporated into a bulls-eye.

Having provided for the parent organization, the service modes were to be identified as subsidiaries. Johnston continued his reporting on modifications for the Underground, Green Line, General, Tramways and Trolleybus logotypes and bulls-eyes, which were to be surcharged with the words 'London' and 'Transport' in the upper and lower counters or semicircles.[19] Letter spacing was the primary focus of the exercise, with Johnston taking full advantage of the fact that the symbols were entirely hand drawn so that 'extreme nicety of adjustment can be achieved' by fine changes.[20] His eye was caught by the close proximity of the new words to the main label in the Waterlow's proofs, which he felt 'spoilt the clean cut structural effect by having this blurred central mass of lettering-plus-label. At the best it becomes a fringed label (reminding me a little of a hairy caterpillar)'.[21] All labels had their white lining thickened to strengthen the overall appearance. The results were later to be criticized by London Transport Publicity Officer Harold Hutchison, who considered the London TransporT label 'a sad lapse' and distortion of the otherwise superb work by Johnston.[22]

By November 1933 the work was nearing completion, and there was some discussion over the colours that might be used for the symbol rings. Johnston evaluated some proofs:

> 3 December 1933. A question arises in my mind as to whether the 'Broad Circle' is sufficiently strong (i.e. broad enough) to carry the label: and this question would be definitely involved in the colour scheme question.[23]

Printers Waterlow and Sons sent their artist J.W. Clarke down to visit Edward Johnston in Ditchling in order to finalize the designs.

One of the London Transport fleet symbols devised to reflect ownership by the parent company.

APPLICATION OF THE SYMBOL

Now we can leave the drawing board in order to consider the implications of all the work undertaken by Edward Johnston, Harry Carr and the Waterlow's artists. In some contexts, including uniform insignia and station name signs, Johnston's designs would survive almost unaltered for three decades. As we will see, in other applications such as posters his work lasted only a few years, and in the case of signs for bus stopping places just a year or two.

Charles Holden viewed the architecture of Underground stations as a project of total design. His brief was gradually extended by Frank Pick so that all aspects of the station environment could be considered as part of the whole, with the bar and circle an important part of the ensemble. The first Underground extension project of the 1920s was to take the Northern line up to Edgware. The five stations, opened 1923–4, were designed by the in-house Underground architects Stanley Heaps and Thomas Bilbow. Their neo-Georgian simplicity included the presentation of Edward Johnston's bar-and-circle symbol in the wrought-iron balustrades over the entrance porticos, or on the walls.

Charles Holden designed new surface entrances for stations on the former City & South London Railway between Elephant & Castle and Angel. Reopened during 1924–5, these projects are interesting because they did *not* feature the bar and circle on their exteriors. Holden instead chose the UndergrounD logotype with larger initial and final letters, crafted in bronze and fixed to the glazed ceramic station façades. Images of Angel reveal a rapid shift in policy, whereby the new station frontage was rebuilt within a year to accommodate a bar-and-circle sign.

Building on the success of these works, Holden obtained the commission to design completely new buildings for the extension of the Northern line beyond Clapham Common to Morden (opened 1926). Made in white Portland stone, the seven stations were fully three-dimensional expositions, complemented by equally bold bar-and-circle signs mounted on 'Venetian' masts to identify the station position to travellers along the street; the arrangement was supposedly inspired by Frank Pick seeing a guardsman holding a sword vertically in Whitehall.

Charles Holden conceived his Morden line station architecture as solidity and mass enclosing flat planes. With an eye for functional decoration, he rendered the bar and circle as a sphere bisected by a block for the column capitals either side of the main vestibule window. In this

As use of the bar and circle advanced across the organization, relatively new buildings were altered at some expense to display the symbol. Angel station, remodelled by Charles Holden, photographed in July 1924 and September 1925, before and after the addition of the bulls-eye to the façade.

Balham Underground station, photographed in August 1927. The bar and circle is the central feature of the ticket-hall window.

window, a coloured glass symbol, recalling medieval cathedrals, ensured that the last thing passengers saw as they rode up the escalators to the surface was the red, white and blue of the Underground.

Sudbury Town (1930–31) was an experimental station, and as such represented an anomaly in any attempt to establish a smooth progression for Holden's station architecture. The opportunity to design a station for this nondescript suburb to the north-west of London made it possible to try out ideas away from the full public gaze. Designed in brick rather than Portland stone, Sudbury Town was a severe and well-proportioned brick box of a building, identified not by a conventional bar and circle but by a two-colour neon-tube logotype combining the form of the UndergrounD logotype with the station name. It is likely that this was modelled directly from Holden's own drawing. The bar and circle did feature in an innovative way at Sudbury Town, in the stained-glass station nameboards set into the booking-hall and waiting-room windows. These are very rare in employing a serif form of the Edward Johnston Railway Block Letter drawn by Percy J. Delf Smith, possibly to explore improved legibility when quick comprehension of the name was important.[24]

We now move on to the northern extension of the Piccadilly line from Finsbury Park to Cockfosters (opened 1932–3). These eight stations, and subsequent Adams, Holden and Pearson commissions built up to 1948, featured an updated form of the Morden line coloured-glass bar and circle in their glazing arrangements and/or flat vitreous-enamel versions mounted onto plinths in the brickwork. Where the buildings had a ground-floor block which projected beyond the main box form, or where there were free-standing passenger shelters outside the stations, three-dimensional box signs were fixed on masts or lighting columns. Buildings with tower features – including Chiswick Park, Turnpike Lane and Bounds Green (all 1932), and Boston Manor and Osterley (both 1934) –

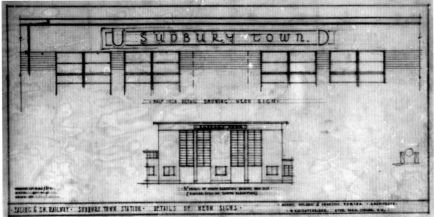

ABOVE: Sudbury Town station platform, photographed in 1932. The bar and circle is incorporated into the booking-hall windows, and the neon sign can be seen at top left.

LEFT: Architect's drawing for the neon-tube name sign at Sudbury Town, a clever adaptation of the Underground logotype to fit the long, shallow space of the concrete roof frieze.

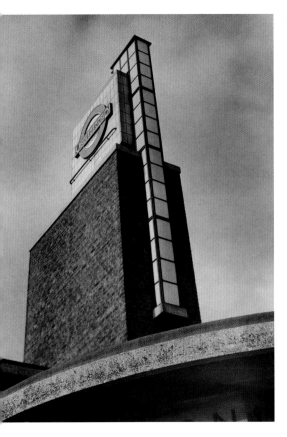

were provided with high-level bar-and-circle symbols made from vitreous enamelled steel, or stained glass which was illuminated from behind at night.

Stations in central London rebuilt during the 1920s and early 1930s featured a curious version of the organization's symbol – a projecting horizontal blue bar with the Underground logotype, but no red ring. Usually this was supplementary to complete signs mounted on the fascia, and occasionally solo bars and bars with circles were combined on the same building. As with the graphical use of the logotype, it is possible that the projecting bars were felt to be more in keeping with the limited space available on stations fitted into a dense streetscape.

When reviewing the cost of developing substantial brick-and-concrete buildings on a system whose traffic was predicted to outgrow facilities every 25 years, London Transport asked Charles Holden to propose a light-weight low-cost form of station building. Essentially shelters for only the most basic needs, these glass-and-steel structures designed during 1936 would have been characterized by a tall mast sign at the roadside, acting as a beacon to travellers.

ABOVE: Illuminated tower at Boston Manor station, designed by Charles Holden with Charles Hutton. The bar and circle is placed at high level to advertise the station over a wide area.

RIGHT: Bounds Green Underground station at the time of opening. On this blustery and wet day, the celebratory banners and bunting add further emphasis to the visual identity conveyed by the bar-and-circle signs fixed to the ticket-hall walls and ventilation tower.

Holborn station, with glass bar and circle in the main window, and open-centred mast-mounted bar-and-circle symbols facing the pedestrians.

The Sloane Street entrance to Knightsbridge station shows the combination of projecting bar UndergrounD logotype signs and bar and circle, used for some of Charles Holden's central London stations. The vertical logos either side of the stairwell entrance are an unusual rendering of the organization's name.

The drive towards unification of London's railways was aided by the use of a common visual identity. The Metropolitan Railway considered itself a main-line company and resisted amalgamation with the Underground Group. It did, however, permit this interpretation by Edward Johnston of its own bar-and-diamond device, produced for Paddington station in 1929.

STATION PLATFORM NAMEBOARDS

The Edward Johnston-designed bar and circle was first adapted for station nameboards in 1923. For surface stations, Charles Holden and his team designed free-standing reinforced-concrete poster displays incorporating bar-and-circle nameboards. Signs were also fixed to the platform walls in tunnel stations, on tiled surrounds or directly to the brickwork. The changes were not system-wide, and some disc-type station nameboards remained in use long after the Second World War – particularly if stations had not been refurbished.

RIGHT, TOP–BOTTOM: Free-standing nameboard at Enfield West (now Oakwood) station, and nameboard fixed directly to the tilework at Wood Green station.

AT THE ROADSIDE

The Underground's building department produced and procured all the signs fixed in London's streets to show where their vehicles stopped to pick up and drop off passengers. A standard form of enamel sign with a curved upper margin was introduced in the early 1920s, to carry the Edward Johnston General and Tramways symbols. Coloured red, blue, cream and black, these stop flags were not consistent throughout the city, but did go some considerable way to presenting the image of a unified system in the otherwise visually busy streetscape. When London Transport took control of the road systems in 1933, stop flags were produced to a revised design. Publicity Officer Harry Carr asked architect Charles Holden to review the design of stopping-place posts and signs. No prototypes were built from these designs. The first intimation of colour coding for road-vehicle networks appeared at this time, with the new flags carrying red, blue or green text blocks to indicate the bus, trolleybus or coach services that served the stops. Tram routes had their own flags, with a different system of coloured graphics to indicate whether vehicles stopped compulsorily or at the passenger's request.

Charles Holden adapted the bar-and-circle symbol for his bus-shelter designs. The shelters were miniature essays in modernism, assembled

The new roadside signs had red, blue and green text blocks to indicate the bus, trolleybus or coach services that served the stops.

Charles Holden-designed bus passenger waiting shelter, photographed when new in 1936.

from enamelled steel and glass without superfluous decoration. In rectangular and circular form, the shelters employed architectural features such as cantilevering, and carried London Transport symbols in their panelling or mounted on masts.

POSTERS

From the 1920s artists began to incorporate the symbol in posters as part of their pictorial compositions. BELOW: 'Time is money, take a season', by Reginald Percy Gossop, 1926; OPPOSITE, CLOCKWISE FROM TOP LEFT: 'The giant stride', by Frederick Charles Herrick, 1922; 'And all for a season ticket on London's Underground', by Frederick Charles Herrick, 1925; 'Why home so soon?', by Mark Fernand Severin, 1938; 'Underground: theatres', by Verney L. Danvers, 1926.

As we saw in the previous chapter, poster artists were given licence to incorporate the trading marks into their overall design scheme. Frequently the label/logotype only would appear, being easier to fit into a block of text. The Johnston logotype featured more frequently on posters from 1926. Where the full symbol was used, the fine lining details of Edward Johnston's originals might be set aside to make bolder versions suited to the visual strength of the poster images. Several artists, including F.C. Herrick and Mark Severin, deconstructed the symbol altogether in order to convey their message.

From 1933 to 1936, the Edward Johnston 'London Transport' bar and circle is common on posters, reproduced in its entirety and in colours to suit the poster. The subsidiary fleet symbols were used too, from time to

THE GIANT STRIDE
FOR A FINE START
AND A FINE HOLIDAY

IT MAY BE A LITTLE HOUSE
BUT THE CAPTIVE AMENITIES —
AND ALL FOR
A SEASON TICKET
ON LONDON'S
UNDERGROUND

Why home so soon?

From 1936, the symbol appeared in increasingly abstracted forms on posters. CLOCKWISE FROM TOP LEFT: 'Spring in the village', by Edward McKnight Kauffer, 1936; 'London in the season', by Walter Goetz, 1938; 'Football', by John Gatrell, 1938; 'Shared joys are doubled', by Mary Adshead, 1937.

time, for specific communications. In this way the bar and circle's presence as a typographical device and a brand mark was confirmed, but this had its own transforming effect on the symbol.

From 1936, Johnston's design rarely featured on pictorial posters. Instead – as a result of the input of designers including Hans Schleger, Edward McKnight Kauffer and László Moholy-Nagy – a seemingly inexhaustible range of abstract forms was seen. All made play of different ways in which the horizontality of the bar and the circularity of the ring might be rendered. By 1939, two versions of the symbol were most common: one in which the bar and ring were shown as fine outlines only, and the other a solid stencil form.

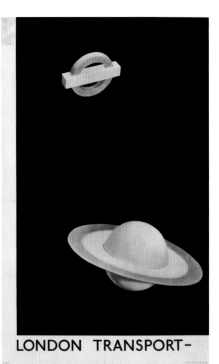

LONDON TRANSPORT-

Radical and mysterious, the bar and circle is rendered in three dimensions as a planet by Man Ray in this 1938 poster, one of a pair.

LEAFLETS AND BOOKLETS

Hundreds of printed paper leaflets and a range of books prompted Londoners and tourists to use Underground Group services for pleasure trips. These small and beautiful objects, often featuring specially commissioned artworks, were issued for particular holiday dates such as Easter or Whitsun, and to coincide with periods of increased shopping, especially Christmas. As the Underground systems were enhanced, leaflets and booklets communicated these changes and achievements to the public. Again, these ephemeral items were colourful examples of innovative graphic design. Artists commissioned for this material made great play of interpreting the bar and circle in imaginative and witty ways.

FOLDER MAPS

Once inspired by posters to make a journey, travellers needed further information to navigate the systems. The most important piece of printed material issued by the Underground Group and its successors was the folder map. Many of us will be familiar with H.C. Beck's tube map, issued to the public as a card folder and printed as a poster for display at stations. Less widely known are the maps produced for the road transport systems – buses, coaches, country buses, trams and trolleybuses. These too came in a convenient pocket size, but folded out into more geographically accurate maps of the capital, with transport services superimposed on the road layout.

As with posters, the bar and circle took many different forms as artists and designers created their own interpretations for other printed publicity. ABOVE, L–R: 'Summer outings and excursions, 1935', leaflet with cover design by John Mansbridge; 'London Town & Country', booklet, 1928.

RIGHT: Each folder map featured a bar and circle on the cover. These changed form over time.

STAFF UNIFORMS

Until 1933, Underground Group uniformed staff had worn various insignia based on the bar and circle. Many men were used to some form of military service, and would have been comfortable wearing a full uniform in peacetime. London Transport knew that successful unification of the company needed to embrace its public-facing workers too, and it devised a set of badges using Edward Johnston's symbol to encourage a sense of belonging among staff. The badges were of two sizes and colour coded. A basic symbol for vehicle crews was produced in blue and white for buses, red for trams and trolleybuses, yellow ochre for railways, and green for country buses and express coaches. Supervisory staff – those who did not operate or support vehicles – wore more ornate insignia designed by silversmith Harold Stabler, incorporating the griffin that appeared on the official London Transport seal. Their badges were similarly colour coded, and produced in either sterling silver or gold-plated silver according to rank.

ABOVE: Posed shot of Underground porter in newly designed uniform, at Lambeth North Railway Training School, 1940.

LEFT, L–R: 'Record of service: General 1931' and 'Record of service: Tramways 1931', posters by Maurice Beck. These men wear various bar-and-circle badges of the period 1913–33.

Hans Schleger (also known as Zero; 1898–1970) came to London from Berlin in 1932. His friend Edward McKnight Kauffer made many introductions for him, and soon Schleger was working on advertising and branding projects for the more progressive design-aware businesses, such as Shell, British Petroleum and the Post Office. Schleger was commissioned by London Transport first as a poster artist, and then asked to review more comprehensively the form of the company's corporate identity (he also redesigned the London Underground railway diagram). Edward Johnston's work was austere, but Schleger brought a combination of witty surrealism and precise minimalism to the London Transport branding. He created a family of symbols based on a plain bar and circle in silhouette (solid) and outline (open) forms. These innovative corporate-identity developments for London Transport set a precedent which has influenced the organization ever since. Very soon, the near monopoly of Edward Johnston designs, which had prevailed for some 15 years, would end.

Hans Schleger's re-imagining of the bulls-eye came out of a London Transport decision to create a system-wide scheme of fixed vehicle-stopping places in 1935.[25] After a commission by Frank Pick, signs used to indicate bus, coach, tram and trolleybus stopping places in the street were radically altered by Schleger. The essence of his brief was a rationalization of signs so that they might be more rapidly recognized by passengers and vehicle crews. For this purpose, his colour palette consisted of red, blue, green, black and white – the colours best differentiated from each other in enamel sign manufacture. Schleger took the basic forms of bar and circle, introduced additional vertical and diagonal motifs, and used the minimum of text. A series of flag designs were fabricated for assessment.[26]

Clever but too abstract, these prototypes gave way once again to the simple clarity of the bar and circle in a second series making direct reference to Schleger's silhouette symbols, which had been drafted for posters. Despite Frank Pick's feeling that they were too modern in appearance, these were approved for use.[27] Their simplicity and efficiency as designed objects is superb. They were shown in red, black and white for buses and trolleybuses; blue, black and white for trams;[28] and green, black and white for long-distance coaches. For signs showing that vehicles could be requested to stop by the traveller raising their arm to the driver, Schleger exploited a feature of surrealism in showing the symbol as a white figure

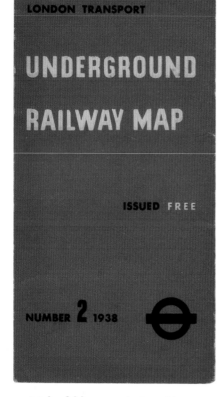

1938 tube folder map designed by Hans Schleger.

ABOVE: Hans Schleger's suite of roadside stop signs, 1936.

RIGHT: Schleger's bus and coach stop flags in situ. Where two services stopped at the same point, two signs were provided. The passenger shelter is to a design by Charles Holden in lightweight vitreous enamel-coated steel and glass.

Streamlined pink terrazzo-concrete post with integral timetable unit, designed by Christian Barman to carry Hans Schleger's new stop signs, 1938. Each post carried a red or green finial to indicate whether buses, coaches, or both served the stop.

on a coloured ground. Where more than one network stopped at the same place, different coloured flags were fixed one above the other. Schleger's stop-flag designs continued in use throughout London until the early 1980s. The changes coincided with the appointment of the architect, industrial designer and journalist Christian Barman as Publicity Officer, and Barman brought his industrial design skills to the project, producing a new terrazzo-concrete bus-stop post with decorative painted finials in 1938, and a second design with integral shelter.

THE CARR–EDWARDS REPORT, 1938

Frank Pick and his teams in the Publicity and Operating departments at London Transport carefully monitored use of the bulls-eye across the service modes, particularly in the environment of the railway station. By the mid-1930s, extension projects for the Piccadilly and Northern lines were completed or in the planning phase. Further sizeable schemes would add to the Central and Bakerloo lines. Interchange traffic between lines was very important for business, accounting for one fifth of all passengers. The need to guide travellers around the increasingly complex Underground required careful control and coordination of signs at railway stations. The ideal – formulated by Frank Pick, Charles Holden, Harry Carr and their operating colleagues – was that the route through the station would be unimpeded by any obstacles, and would be the most efficient one possible. Experiments were carried out using full-size mock-ups of station entrances, ticket halls and passageways to the platforms. By doing this, Pick and his colleagues were able to explore the passenger experience of passing from street to train, and to consider the signs that they would need along the way.

To walk the route for ourselves, the first sight of the station would be the exterior mast- or post-mounted three-dimensional bulls-eye. Moving closer, a horizontal strip of blue carried white lettering for the station name, available lines and small bulls-eyes. Inside the ticket hall, the free-standing 'passimeter' kiosk, from which tickets were issued, would carry a small bar and circle with the station name. At the point where the level changed to access the platforms, further two- or three-dimensional symbols showed the way. On reaching platform level, the platform numbers were indicated with bulls-eye symbols, and route maps carried the device as well.[29] The platform walls displayed both large station nameboards and, in the case of tunnel stations, horizontal friezes

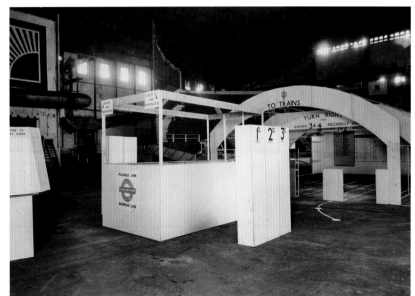

Full-size mock-ups developing the signage needed for the journey taken by the passenger from street to train.

with station names and bulls-eyes. Small station-name bulls-eyes would be fitted at regular intervals on the wall facing the platform. Further trademarks featured in the decoration: Harold Stabler of the Poole Pottery designed ceramic tiles with the bulls-eye motif, and London Transport architects devised a clock on which the hours were marked by miniature symbols. Even inside the tube carriage, the passenger was reminded of the operator's brand by the graphics associated with line diagrams.

Harry Carr and W.P.N. Edwards, Lord Ashfield's secretary, were assigned to study the use of way-finding signs on the system. They encountered many different uses of the bulls-eye symbol, in every type of sign. The most prevalent adaptation was for direction arrows, on which the bar of the symbol was transformed into an arrow piercing the circle. In another variation, a line of text replaced the bar entirely, and in yet a third form, both arrow and text were combined. There was a bulls-eye with an arrow fitted into the blue bar, and other odd applications for platform number signs. Chancery Lane (Central line) was unique in having a single sign with blocky bulls-eye/arrow symbol. St Paul's (formerly Post Office, Central line) had signs a lighter blue than usual, changing the colour scheme of the direction arrows.

Following their survey work, Carr and Edwards produced a report in 1938 that summarized their experiments, and which was effectively the first London Transport corporate identity manual.[30] In what seems in

In the 1930s London Transport signwriters created several ingenious variations on the bulls-eye symbol for directional signs.

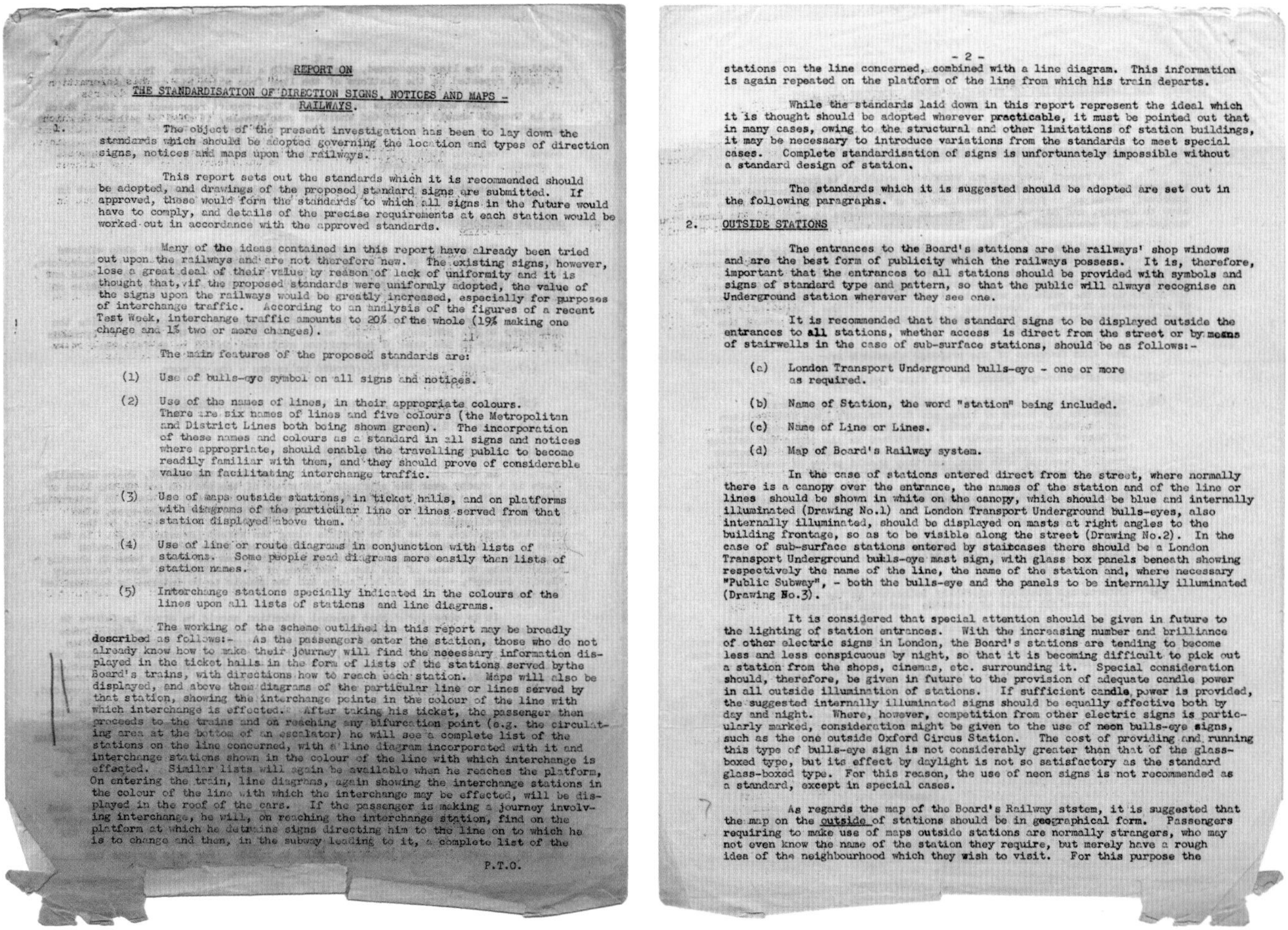

REPORT ON

THE STANDARDISATION OF DIRECTION SIGNS, NOTICES AND MAPS - RAILWAYS.

1. The object of the present investigation has been to lay down the standards which should be adopted governing the location and types of direction signs, notices and maps upon the railways.

This report sets out the standards which it is recommended should be adopted, and drawings of the proposed standard signs are submitted. If approved, these would form the standards to which all signs in the future would have to comply, and details of the precise requirements at each station would be worked out in accordance with the approved standards.

Many of the ideas contained in this report have already been tried out upon the railways and are not therefore new. The existing signs, however, lose a great deal of their value by reason of lack of uniformity and it is thought that, if the proposed standards were uniformly adopted, the value of the signs upon the railways would be greatly increased, especially for purposes of interchange traffic. According to an analysis of the figures of a recent Test Week, interchange traffic amounts to 20% of the whole (19% making one change and 1% two or more changes).

The main features of the proposed standards are:

(1) Use of bulls-eye symbol on all signs and notices.

(2) Use of the names of lines, in their appropriate colours. There are six names of lines and five colours (the Metropolitan and District Lines both being shown green). The incorporation of these names and colours as a standard in all signs and notices where appropriate, should enable the travelling public to become readily familiar with them, and they should prove of considerable value in facilitating interchange traffic.

(3) Use of maps outside stations, in ticket halls, and on platforms with diagrams of the particular line or lines served from that station displayed above them.

(4) Use of line or route diagrams in conjunction with lists of stations. Some people read diagrams more easily than lists of station names.

(5) Interchange stations specially indicated in the colours of the lines upon all lists of stations and line diagrams.

The working of the scheme outlined in this report may be broadly described as follows:- As the passengers enter the station, those who do not already know how to make their journey will find the necessary information displayed in the ticket halls in the form of lists of the stations served by the Board's trains, with directions how to reach each station. Maps will also be displayed, and above them diagrams of the particular line or lines served by that station, showing the interchange points in the colour of the line with which interchange is effected. After taking his ticket, the passenger then proceeds to the trains and on reaching any bifurcation point (e.g. the circulating area at the bottom of an escalator) he will see a complete list of the stations on the line concerned, with a line diagram incorporated with it and interchange stations shown in the colour of the line with which interchange is effected. Similar lists will again be available when he reaches the platform, On entering the train, line diagrams, again showing the interchange stations in the colour of the line with which the interchange may be effected, will be displayed in the roof of the cars. If the passenger is making a journey involving interchange, he will, on reaching the interchange station, find on the platform at which he detrains signs directing him to the line on to which he is to change and then, in the subway leading to it, a complete list of the

P.T.O.

- 2 -

stations on the line concerned, combined with a line diagram. This information is again repeated on the platform of the line from which his train departs.

While the standards laid down in this report represent the ideal which it is thought should be adopted wherever practicable, it must be pointed out that in many cases, owing to the structural and other limitations of station buildings, it may be necessary to introduce variations from the standards to meet special cases. Complete standardisation of signs is unfortunately impossible without a standard design of station.

The standards which it is suggested should be adopted are set out in the following paragraphs.

2. OUTSIDE STATIONS

The entrances to the Board's stations are the railways' shop windows and are the best form of publicity which the railways possess. It is, therefore, important that the entrances to all stations should be provided with symbols and signs of standard type and pattern, so that the public will always recognise an Underground station wherever they see one.

It is recommended that the standard signs to be displayed outside the entrances to **all** stations, whether access is direct from the street or by means of stairwells in the case of sub-surface stations, should be as follows:-

(a) London Transport Underground bulls-eye - one or more as required.

(b) Name of Station, the word "station" being included.

(c) Name of Line or Lines.

(d) Map of Board's Railway system.

In the case of stations entered direct from the street, where normally there is a canopy over the entrance, the names of the station and of the line or lines should be shown in white on the canopy, which should be blue and internally illuminated (Drawing No.1) and London Transport Underground bulls-eyes, also internally illuminated, should be displayed on masts at right angles to the building frontage, so as to be visible along the street (Drawing No.2). In the case of sub-surface stations entered by staircases there should be a London Transport Underground bulls-eye mast sign, with glass box panels beneath showing respectively the name of the line, the name of the station and, where necessary "Public Subway", - both the bulls-eye and the panels to be internally illuminated (Drawing No.3).

It is considered that special attention should be given in future to the lighting of station entrances. With the increasing number and brilliance of other electric signs in London, the Board's stations are tending to become less and less conspicuous by night, so that it is becoming difficult to pick out a station from the shops, cinemas, etc. surrounding it. Special consideration should, therefore, be given in future to the provision of adequate candle power in all outside illumination of stations. If sufficient candle power is provided, the suggested internally illuminated signs should be equally effective both by day and night. Where, however, competition from other electric signs is particularly marked, consideration might be given to the use of neon bulls-eye signs, such as the one outside Oxford Circus Station. The cost of providing and running this type of bulls-eye sign is not considerably greater than that of the glass-boxed type, but its effect by daylight is not so satisfactory as the standard glass-boxed type. For this reason, the use of neon signs is not recommended as a standard, except in special cases.

As regards the map of the Board's Railway ststem, it is suggested that the map on the <u>outside</u> of stations should be in geographical form. Passengers requiring to make use of maps outside stations are normally strangers, who may not even know the name of the station they require, but merely have a rough idea of the neighbourhood which they wish to visit. For this purpose the

retrospect to be an overworked exercise, the report advocated the use of bulls-eye symbols on all signs and notices. This would be completed at certain Central line stations designed before – but opened after – the war, but greater proliferation of the bulls-eye would have to wait until after 1945. As we will see in Chapter 4, the Carr–Edwards Report was reviewed critically and its recommendations reigned in.

At this point, with more than a decade of intensive activity behind us, we look at how the bulls-eye symbol served as a totem of national identity, courage and homeland during the Second World War.

The 1938 Carr–Edwards Report proposed a standard system of sign provision at Underground stations. Many of the signs would feature the bar and circle.

'Be punctual', poster by Tom Eckersley, 1945.

3

THE SYMBOL GOES TO WAR

For the Underground during the First World War (1914–18) and for London Transport through the Second World War (1939–45), participation in the conflict took place on many levels. The bar-and-circle symbol had an important role in this context. It was used to identify communications with the public, and with transport staff. The symbol was worn by service operators and created a sense of camaraderie for the non-actively combatant personnel, including the thousands of women recruited to replace the men who had gone to war. Staff involved in voluntary war work – be it the manufacture of fighting equipment, work on food production or distribution, or the administration of air-raid shelters – all carried the bar and circle in the public realm.

During the First World War, Underground posters urged men to sign up for military service. The London General Omnibus Company sent over

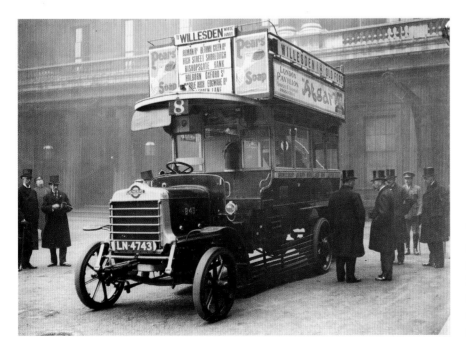

The bus nicknamed 'Old Bill', one of many London buses used overseas during the First World War, being inspected by King George V after restoration in 1920. The bar and circle on the front of the vehicle took the symbol to Europe for the first time.

'Help the conductor', sticker by Toni del Renzio, 1945.

Troops carried the London Transport logo into war with this tactical sign for the Royal Army Service Corps, *c*. 1940.

<small>RIGHT:</small> 'A woman's job in war', poster, 1941.

1,300 passenger buses into battle alongside the Army Service Corps, the vehicles converted to move troops, the wounded, equipment or carrier pigeons. Each bus serving in France or Belgium reminded troops of London and Britain, and many carried the General's bar and circle. One bus returned to be feted for its war service, and consequently the bar and circle was placed alongside the names of notorious battles, the tragedies and achievements of the fighting. Nicknamed 'Old Bill', the bus made an official visit to Buckingham Palace to be inspected by King George V, and took part in both regular services in London and Armistice Day parades from 1920 until 1970. 'Old Bill' is now in the Imperial War Museum, London.

When war broke out in Europe in 1939, London Transport had to set aside its second five-year New Works Plan of extensions and alterations to rail and road networks, and divert resources to the war effort. Unfinished projects were adapted for new uses, and all unnecessary travel was discouraged. Male staff joined the armed forces, and women again returned to transport operation. London Transport formed an anti-aircraft battery and built aeroplanes.

PROPAGANDA AND INFORMATION

London Transport had a perfect display space adjacent to the ticket hall at Charing Cross (now Embankment) station, at which to speak to the public on war-related topics. In the first year of hostilities, it began a series of photographic exhibitions aimed at boosting morale and explaining the conflict. The bulls-eye symbol featured in the many official posters and leaflets issued for instructive and propaganda purposes, and it was proudly and affectionately used in informal ways as a totem of unity, service, reliability and continuity.

Christian Barman left London Transport in 1941, and Frank Pick died the same year, having resigned in 1940. Harry Carr took charge of a much-reduced publicity programme. Hans Schleger's work for London Transport continued through the Second World War, when the visual economy of his designs made them appropriate for a period of utility and thrift. With intense air raids over Britain during the Blitz of 1940–41, the Second World War affected the civilian population greatly. The blackout – official limiting of light emission by buildings, street lamps and vehicles at night to confuse enemy aircraft – made travel difficult. A series of posters used the bulls-eye in ingenious ways to inform the public about

THIS PAGE: Posters encouraging safer use of public transport during the blackout. CLOCKWISE FROM TOP LEFT: 'In the blackout: A flashing torch is dangerous', by Bruce Angrave, 1942; 'Inside it's bright, outside it's dark', by James Fitton, 1941; 'In the blackout: Before you alight make sure the train is in the station', by Hans Schleger (Zero), 1943.

OPPOSITE: Posters by James Fitton relating London Transport's activities in support of the war effort or asking for public cooperation, with the bar and circle as a vital and unbreakable link. CLOCKWISE FROM TOP LEFT: 'Rubber is precious; travel only when you must'; 'Steering London through daylight and blackout'; 'Your goodwill eases our daily task'; 'Linking home and factory; turning the wheels of war' (all 1943).

Rubber is precious

Travel only when you must

Steering London through

daylight & blackout - faithfully

Linking home and factory

Turning the wheels of war

Your goodwill eases

our daily task

Bill Store

ABOVE: The London Transport staff magazine *Pennyfare* made friendly propaganda of the symbol in the form of these cartoon characters.

BELOW: Prisoners of war in the Stalag 383, Hohenfels, Bavaria, with their mascot – a painted symbol of their employer at home.

RIGHT: 'London Transport', the first Spitfire financed by the London Transport Spitfire Fund, to which the staff contributed. Photographed 1942.

safer use of public transport after dark. London Transport formed units of Local Defence Volunteers, which became seven battalions of Home Guard.[1] Subterranean railway tunnels began to be used as air-raid shelters, and others were converted to factories for the production of necessary equipment. Further posters urged the public, and London Transport's own employees, to save resources and increase their energies in contributing to the war effort. Other printed material reminded London of the vital service being given by those involved in the transport system. London Transport's staff magazine, *Pennyfare*, continued to be published throughout the war to reduced specification. It was circulated throughout the organization and sent to all employees serving in the armed forces around

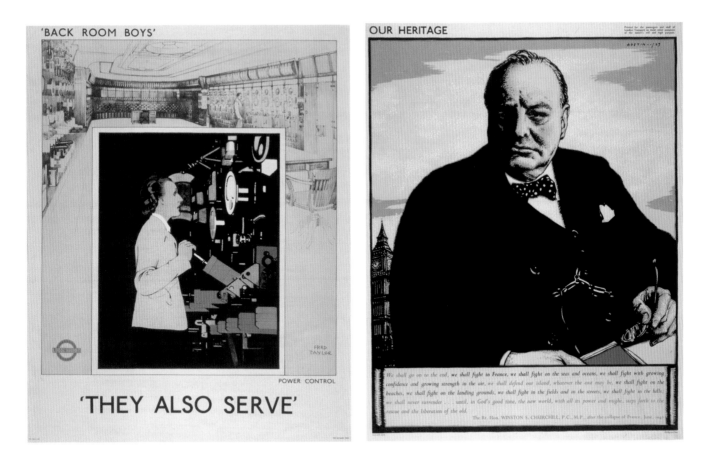

the world. *Pennyfare* carried several stories of the bulls-eye as a propaganda device, accompanying troops across the desert and uniting prisoners of war. It appeared in cartoons, posters and even on the two Spitfire aircraft funded entirely by contributions from transport employees.

The Western Allies invaded Fascist Italy in 1943 and France in 1944. Posters displayed at London Transport locations placed the symbol in the context of messages to endure, and to remember the homeland. Walter Spradbery's *Proud City* series was printed in Arabic and Farsi, taking the bar and circle to far-off theatres of war. This visibility reminded soldiers of home. An unofficial and yet significant manifestation of the London Transport logo was in battle itself. It was painted onto tanks, and correspondence in the staff magazine *Pennyfare* noted: 'One of our signs, that of Angel station, has been adopted as the emblem of a London battery overseas.' The Light Anti-Aircraft Battery was based in Penton Street, Islington, near to the Northern line station, and chose the bulls-eye to identify itself. Copies of this sign were taken overseas in 1941, to the north of Persia [Iran]. The sign then went with the troops through 'Iraq,

ABOVE, L–R: 'Back room boys, they also serve: power control', poster by Fred Taylor, 1942; 'Our heritage: Winston Churchill', poster by Robert Sargent Austin, 1943.

Posters from the series 'The Proud City' by Walter E. Spradbery (1944) were printed in Arabic and Farsi. L—R: 'St Paul's Cathedral' (Arabic version); 'The Temple Church and library after bombardment' (Farsi version).

Palestine, Trans-Jordan, Egypt and Libya', across the Mediterranean Sea and through the allied forces' landing into Sicily, carried on men's backs. One sergeant in the battery wrote: 'Very soon, the sign will be taken many hundreds of miles again. Shrapnel smashed my copy; but I've got a new one, ready for the next job. And you would be surprised at the interest the sign causes when seen for the first time'.[2] Captured soldiers, too, were proud of their employer's totem: 'Sixteen prisoners in the Stalag 383, Bavaria, share a bond of fellowship above and beyond that of captivity in the same camp. They are all London Transport men. They went so far as to paint a copy of the London Transport bulls-eye sign.'[3] Bomber aeroplanes were informally manufactured in buildings intended for railway-car maintenance, their production identified by a bulls-eye with wings. When war ended in 1945, James Fitton crafted important statistics into engaging graphics based on the bulls-eye, while Fred Taylor informed the public of efforts to restore the transport system to full operation. An international audience of service personnel and politicians would have seen the bulls-eye elevated alongside the flags of 34 countries, in Austin Cooper's celebration of the United Nations' founding in 1945. With the return of peace, the bar and circle was set for renewed challenges and purposes to advance its evolution.

REHABILITATION

For the protection of passengers
137 anti-blast walls were placed at the entrances
to 75 stations. These walls are being demolished
as quickly as possible — but

IT TAKES TIME

THEY · SHOUT · FOR · JOY · THEY · ALSO · SING

PASSENGERS

In 1944 when London's transport needs were greatest

BUS

1,896 million
520 million
956 million

RAILWAY

TROLLEYBUS AND TRAM

passengers were carried by London Transport

CARRIES ON

LONDON TRANSPORT
STAFF REUNION
VICTORY DINNER

CONNAUGHT ROOMS
3rd and 10th July 1946

ABOVE, L–R: 'Rehabilitation, it takes time: anti-blast', poster by Fred Taylor, 1945; 'They shout for joy, they also sing: flags of allied nations', poster by Austin Cooper, 1944.

RIGHT, L–R: 'Passengers: London Transport carries on', poster by James Fitton, 1945; for the staff reunion dinner in July 1946, the bulls-eye became a symbol of victory.

'Go by Green Line to the Festival', poster by Hans Unger, 1950, for the 1951 Festival of Britain.

4

ART FOR ALL

THE ADVERTISING AGENCY MAN

In 1947, reassembling itself from war and preparing for the move into state ownership, the London Passenger Transport Board – which now had to proceed without several of its creators in Frank Pick (died 1941), Edward Johnston (died 1944), Harry Carr (retired 1946) and Lord Ashfield (resigned 1947, died 1948) – appointed a man from the advertising industry to lead its publicity. This outsider, Harold F. Hutchison, would make changes to every aspect of the organization's visual identity. Hutchison's central role in directing the visual appearance of London's transport is the focus of this chapter.

Through his work as Publicity Officer, Hutchison would position the organization as the pre-eminent face of London, alongside the Houses of Parliament, royalty, the London policeman and the red telephone box. He would reaffirm the value of the inter-war publicity team, increasing the output of printed material and extending the use of the corporate symbol. Every object, place and activity would bear the bar-and-circle brand mark. Caught up with the spirit of post-war reform, and working with a new generation of artists and designers, he had a clear ambition to change the public face of London Transport. With hindsight, it can be appreciated that Hutchison steered a difficult course between modernity and tradition in order to attract, enthral and inform visitors and citizens, to entice shoppers and deter rush-hour travellers, and to promote city and country.

Hutchison had handled the advertising account for Unilever, and directed advertising campaigns for the Empire Marketing Board, the Post Office Telephone Service and the wartime Ministry of Food. With this experience of selling goods and utilities to the public, he was well equipped for marketing London's transport networks to individual households and on a global scale. Reflecting the spirit of Hutchison's background, this chapter is presented as a series of campaigns across a diverse range of activities and situations, to show how the bulls-eye symbol evolved and led the organization.

'The Publicity Office was responsible for gently reminding the public that here was the finest urban transport system in the world.'
BRYCE BEAUMONT[1]

Post-war reconstruction brought Britain into the mindset of modernity in a way which had, pre-war, been evident only in a limited number of infrastructural and architectural projects for enlightened and progressive clients. A programme of updating and streamlining the form and appearance of almost everything in the public and private realms gave space for new expression in art and design, and a rejection of seemingly outdated styles. Under Harold Hutchison, London Transport strove to celebrate its heritage and modernize its image.

London was subject to substantial rebuilding projects, the bombs having achieved a scale of demolition that visionary planners could only have dreamt of before the war. Buildings, roads and whole urban quarters changed, calling for alterations and additions to transport services. To accommodate 'overspill' populations displaced by the war, several New Towns were designated around the metropolis.[2] London Transport would extend its networks in and around these locations. The replacement

Map covers specially designed for the 1948 Olympic Games, the 1951 Festival of Britain and the Coronation of Elizabeth II in 1953.

London buses provided the official transport for organizers and competitors at the 1948 London Olympic Games.

of London's tramway and trolleybus networks by oil-engined buses in 1952 and 1962 respectively, changed how the systems were marketed. Routemaster, the new purpose-designed London bus, was introduced in 1956, while the first new Underground line for many years opened as the Victoria line during 1968–71.

Events related to affairs of state would bring the bulls-eye symbol into many different situations throughout Harold Hutchison's time in his post. London hosted its second Olympic Games in 1948. The Festival of Britain (1951) and the Coronation of Her Majesty Queen Elizabeth II in 1953 also required special transport services and accompanying publicity.

In the area of design, the Council of Industrial Design (CoID; now the Design Council) had been set up by the British wartime government in 1944 to advance better standards of products. The CoID was instrumental in the 'Britain Can Make It' exhibition of 1946, and the Festival of Britain in 1951. The function and appearance of things was increasingly part of a wider debate, although it remained – and remains – a challenge for industry to combine these two aspects of man-made objects. Private agencies such as Design Research Unit (DRU, formed 1943) and Terence Conran's Design Group (1956) worked as multidisciplinary architectural/graphic/industrial design teams to address projects in more holistic ways. DRU was later appointed consultant to London Transport (see Chapter 5).

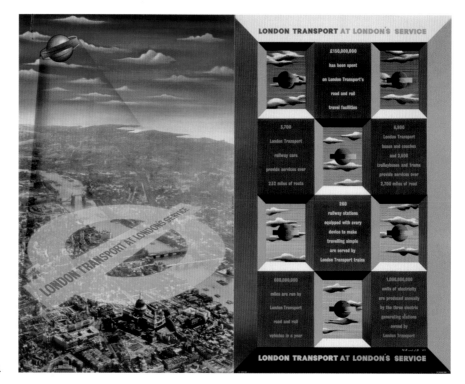

'London Transport at London's service', poster by Misha Black and John Rowland Barker (known as Kraber), 1947.

Staff shortages after the Second World War saw the bulls-eye travelling to countries including Ireland (from 1950) and Barbados (from 1956) to recruit London Transport workers. After a strike by London bus workers in 1958, publicity was required to bring passengers back to public transport in the face of increased private car ownership. Even as indigenous travellers considered their transport options, the inception of airborne mass tourism gave London Transport a significant new audience to understand and communicate with. After the war, the company revived the slogan 'At London's Service' to convey the fundamental purpose of all its activities.

LONDON TRANSPORT, BRITISH TRANSPORT

The bringing together into national ownership of transport systems under the British Transport Commission in 1948 took the bulls-eye symbol beyond London. In its rare direct communications with the public, this new entity called itself *British Transport*. The commission was led by Lord Cyril Hurcomb, who made it his business to procure a trading symbol. Historical precedents had demonstrated the importance of identifying marks with which to advance a project of renewal and

84

merger. There were close links with London Transport: Hurcomb was a friend of Lord Ashfield, while Ashfield was briefly a member of the commission. Former London Transport Publicity Officer Christian Barman was Chief Publicity Officer to the Commission, and would later be a member of the British Railways Design Panel, which worked to improve and unify all aspects of the railway network. So it followed that the British Transport Commission looked for ideas on how to unite its constituents. London Transport was asked to comment on proposed trademarks for the new main-line railway operating organization, but declined. In its full form, the device was complex and ungainly, drawing together many visual references to transport in an attempt to produce a modern yet symbolic trademark, which was supposed to express the authority and wide scope of the commission's responsibilities. The commission issued this insignia to its uniformed railway officers and displayed it on vehicles.

But there was a complication: the parent organization comprised separate executives: those for London Transport, the Railways, Road Services, Docks & Inland Waterways, and Hotels. London Transport determinedly retained its bar and circle, and the other executives tried to find individual symbols to identify their activities. The Railway Executive had a clear sense of itself, being formed from four large and confident national railway networks. Michael Bonavia, a railway historian close to the senior management of British Railways, was clear that Lord Ashfield would not have offered the symbol to the executives of the British Transport Commission.[3] Bonavia argued that other railway operators had already demonstrated how totem devices could be used successfully – the Southern, Metropolitan, and London and North Eastern railways being examples – and that if there was any direct connection it was Lord Ashfield reminding the commission of his success with the bulls-eye. Former London and North Eastern Railway Advertising Manager A.J. White became the Railway Executive's Advertising Officer. He coordinated the branding of the six regional divisions of the Railway Executive, continuing the use of the Gill sans fount begun by his former employer and devising his own totem for railway use.[4]

A second response to the commission's unfortunate device was that a Leslie Marson of the Development and Works Office drew symbols of a bar-and-circle form for several applications: 'a locomotive wheel centre for the Railway Executive, a lorry wheel for the Road Transport Executive, and a lifebelt for the Docks and Inland Waterways Executive.'[5] These proposals influenced the symbols used by the businesses in their first few years. A similar logo was taken up by Midland Red Motorbus services.

The lion-and-wheel symbol, derived from the London Transport bar and circle to represent the newly nationalized transport networks in Britain, 1948.

BRITISH RAILWAYS TOTEM

A.J. White's totem symbol for British Railways suggested a compressed bar and circle.

Several transport systems created logos based on the London Transport symbol. FROM TOP: The Docks & Inland Waterways Executive of the British Transport Commission; Midland Red motor buses; and Córas Iompair Éireann, the Irish state railway system. All mid-1950s.

Córas Iompair Éireann, the railway system of the Irish state, created its own bar and circle.

THE BATTLE FOR UndergrounD

Harold Hutchison was an amateur biographer of English monarchs; considering the modernization of London Transport, he said, 'every new reign must turn its back on the old'.[6] This statement came towards the end of a two-year review into the naming of the railway system: a debate between traditionalists and progressives which threatened the fundamental identity of the system for which the bar-and-circle bulls-eye was the chief envoy. For almost four decades, the main provider of rail and road services in London had been coordinated by the Underground Electric Railways. Since 1908, it had used the title *Underground* on much of its advertising and publicity – as a rectangular name label or logotype, and on the bar-and-circle symbol.

As we saw in Chapter 2, the first move away from sole use of *Underground* in marketing the transport network occurred in 1933, when Frank Pick commissioned Edward Johnston to add *London Transport* – the trading name of the London Passenger Transport Board – to the bar and circle. Even though the organization was no longer legally known as the Underground, Pick retained the word for publicity on the railway system, not least because of the incredible effort he had put into promoting the name since 1908. The series of new stations designed in 1932–3 by Charles Holden and his team carried the *Underground* name: to dispense with it so quickly would have been difficult to justify financially. As a compromise, Pick had commissioned a family of symbols to which the words *London* and *Transport* were added in the half circles. Hans Schleger removed all text from the symbol in 1935–6, producing two powerful versions used to brand the organization during wartime, and to announce its first post-war accomplishments.

In 1947, with the London Passenger Transport Board soon to pass into state ownership, Chairman Lord Ashfield had stated that the title *London Transport* should replace the word *Underground* on signs across the railway system 'as circumstances and supplies permit'. The name was gradually removed from printed publicity, vehicles and station interiors.[7] As initiator of the original UndergrounD brand in 1908, Ashfield may have felt it was within his remit to order the change. Following nationalization, was it now possible to complete the visual rebranding of the system?

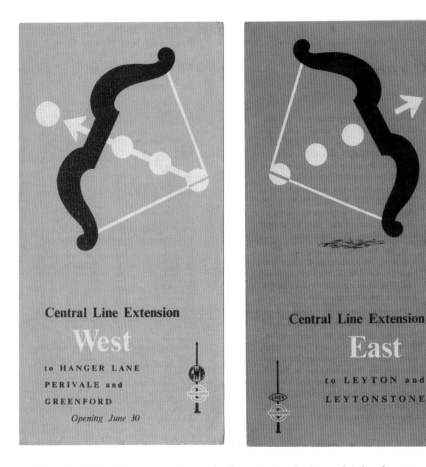

Central Line Extension

West

to HANGER LANE
PERIVALE and
GREENFORD

Opening June 30

Central Line Extension

East

to LEYTON and
LEYTONSTONE

Leaflets designed by Hans Schleger (Zero) to publicize the extensions to the Central Line that opened in 1947. Here the London Transport symbol is shown alongside the monograms of two main-line railway companies, demonstrating the trend for such logotypes at this time.

Harold Hutchison reviewed the symbols by which the London Transport railway system was identified.[8] Predicated on the possibility of abandoning altogether the use of the word *Underground*, to give 'the utmost publicity to the words "London Transport"', this review was a thorough and cogently argued study. While Lord Ashfield had set the review in motion, he died in 1948 and there emerged divided and emotive opinions, not least because many of the organization's officers had come into the business when it *was* the Underground.

To allay the objections of traditionalists, Hutchison evaluated the historical worth and future value of the title *Underground*, and 'the enormous goodwill behind the word' with the travelling public.[9] He found that 'a name with so old and so famous a tradition, with a significance so securely established, with a meaning so precise (it says "London's electric underground trains and stations" in one word), is not lightly to be discarded, even though its typography and design may badly need purification'.[10]

On the progressive side, he noted that the *London Transport* brand had accrued much of its positive reputation since 1933 by association with and by use alongside *Underground* on signs and publicity. Furthermore, while *Underground* was now technically and legally incorrect, it was also 'an

London Transport bulls-eye (TOP), and the lined fleet bulls-eyes for Green Line, Railways, and Trolleybus and Tram (all 1948).

inaccuracy which links with the past and not the present or future'.[11] A compromise was indicated: 'there seems to be both logic and progress in maintaining a symbol which for so long has said "trains", taking it away from a title which is no longer a title of anything ... Is it sound economics at this juncture of our history to devote this space [on the mass of signs all over the railway system] to linking our symbol with its disused past?'[12]

Having noted that the bus and coach networks were comprehensively identified as London Transport facilities, the main problem was the appropriate identification of stations. Should stations be labelled *Underground* because they always had been marked in this way, or *London Transport* because that was who they belonged to – or should they follow the example of railway-platform signs in carrying the name of the station, in order to become useful geographical landmarks? Should the significant value of advertising space outside railway stations be linked with a redundant name?

Despite intensive studies, Hutchison's final report reiterated the dilemma that the Senior Manager of the London Transport Railways division still wanted to retain the title *Underground* on bar-and-circle signs as the traditional identifier of the system. Practical testing of the ideas followed, and these directed the evolution of the bulls-eye. There were two contexts for the main changes, on printed items and outside railway stations. The outcome was a compromise, with Hutchison's recommendations and the wishes of the railway operating department combined.

GRAPHIC MODERNIZATION

Hutchison believed that the London Transport typography and design 'may badly need purification', and he said that Johnston's *Underground* name label was 'a disaster ... now recognised as a sad lapse'.[13] By 1947, the family of symbols devised by Edward Johnston had been restyled with equal-height lettering and the hyphen dashes removed. Lining to the rings was reduced in 1948, and all outlining abandoned in 1949. Alongside the emphasis on a single operating name, in accordance with policy changes, the Underground Diagram of Lines was retitled 'Railways' in 1948. Curiously, the emphasis on transport *mode* rather than fleet *name* did not extend to system maps and other printed material, which continued to be identified with dedicated symbols: Green Line, Tram, Trolleybus, Trolleybus & Tram, or Bus.[14]

BUS MAP
COUNTRY AREA

With the Compliments
LONDON

GREEN LINE
COACH MAP
FREE
1948
ON TRANSPORT
EXECUTIVE
BROADWAY, S.W.1
ABBEY 1234

RAILWAYS
RAM OF LINES

BUS MAP
CENTRAL AREA
INCLUDING TROLLEYBUSES

With the Compliments of
LONDON TRANSPORT
55 BROADWAY, S.W.1
ABBEY 1234

1957

TROLLEYBUS & TRAM
ROUTE MAP

Folder maps for the rail, bus, country bus, express coach, tram and trolleybus networks carried a series of bulls-eyes reflecting the graphic changes from 1948 to 1957.

The lack of uniformity in signs across the organization had increased during the war. In an attempt to engender more consistent marking of buildings and services, the 1948 *Brochure of Standard Drawings* was developed from the Carr–Edwards Report of 1938 (see Chapter 2), with successive editions of a *Standard Sign Manual* circulated in 1951, 1954, 1959 and 1964 as changes were made to the style of signs.

Mast signs – to be seen from a distance along the street, marking the position of a London Transport station – presented the main difficulty. Should they carry *Underground*, *London Transport*, or the station name? The red, white and blue symbol was sufficiently established in the streetscape to infer *Underground* – both 'station' and 'railway' – at a distance. Hutchison recommended abandoning the word *Underground* on these signs. However, showing *London Transport* here would add nothing to the visual information available, so the ideal solution was to apply the station name to the mast symbol. (He had thought about retaining the words *London* and *Transport* in the white counters of the signs, as had been the practice since 1933, but finally rejected this as typographically poor.)[15] Other London Transport premises for buses and coaches would carry the geographical name and the word 'garage' or 'depot' as appropriate. The façade sign on the front of the building should give the correct name of the organization: 'London Transport'. The canopy sign over the entrance would show the station name and the names of the lines available. Signs inside the stations underwent partial modernization too. Where rebuilding or repair called for new station nameboards, these were rendered with plain rings and bars. Continuous strip signs or 'friezes' above the advertising posters on subsurface and deep-level railway platforms featured colour-coded bulls-eyes and borders to indicate the lines serving the platform.[16]

Continuous strip signs or 'friezes', decorated with bar-and-circle symbols in the line colours, were placed above the poster panels on subsurface and deep-level railway platforms to aid passenger recognition.

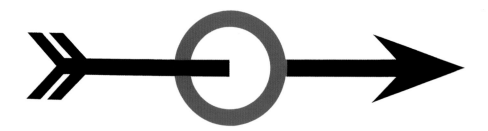

Directional arrows were simplified from 1949.

ABOVE: Some mast signs installed at new stations on the Central line extensions (opened 1947–8) carried London Transport on the masts (e.g. Leyton), while others showed the station name (e.g. Hainault). Both types showed the line name in the counters, a divergence from Hutchison's proposals. At Hanger Lane and Sloane Square the counters were dispensed with altogether, producing particularly elegant signs in a form first developed by architect Charles Holden in the 1920s. Where stations were accessed only by stairwells, the symbol would show the name London Transport on the bar, with a separate illuminated sign beneath it bearing the station name.

ABOVE: Harold Hutchison had a tendency to complicate matters, and his ideas for re-signing the system would mean that the bar and circle had to be supplemented by other information. The only way to achieve this was by providing a minimum number of three different signs: signs on the front of stations, signs on the canopies over station entrances, and signs on masts projecting from the station fronts or canopies.

Detailed analysis of London Transport's publicity gave Harold Hutchison the opportunity to celebrate its considerable achievements, at a critical moment when the organization was being subsumed into a much bigger and less well-defined state structure: 'in these early days of nationalization, it seems the right moment to review the poster-art of these forty years in order that so distinguished a heritage may be neither lost nor disowned.'[17] Opened by the Prime Minister Clement (later Lord) Attlee, the exhibition 'Art for All' at the Victoria and Albert Museum, London, from April to July 1949, featured 40 years of underground posters, shown in partnership with the artworks from which they were produced and a range of related artefacts. A second presentation of London Transport design was staged at the Royal Institute of British Architects, London, in 1951. 'A Centenary Exhibition of London Transport Posters' – at the Royal Institute of Painters in Water Colours Galleries, London, in 1963 brought together many of the artists and designers then active on poster work.

Hutchison's great innovation in poster design was to free artists from the need to incorporate text in their artworks. This was achieved by

'The Seen', pair poster by James Fitton, 1948.

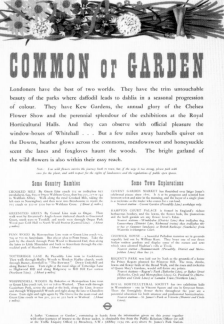

'Common or garden', pair poster by Edwin Tatum, 1954.

'City', pair poster by Edward Bawden, 1952.

A psychology pstudent of Pstaines
Psaid his ego was pshattered by trains
Pso he took it to psee
The pceremony
Of Changing the Guard which takes place every morning
at the Horse Guards and on most mornings at
Buckingham Palace or St. James's. All the details
are contained in a leaflet, obtainable free from the
Publicity Officer, London Transport, 55 Broadway, S.W.1.

'Changing of the Guard', poster by
Frederic Henri Kay Henrion, 1956.

reviving the pre-war practice of commissioning 'pair posters': two printed sheets of double-royal size to be mounted side by side or in close proximity. One would feature a largely pictorial design, and the other would carry the majority of the publicity copy and other graphic information. There was no strict policy on use of the bulls-eye: the Publicity Officer took a 'horses for courses' approach, selecting the best version for the task: an outline or a solid version, depending upon the design context, in order to balance the image and text. Artists incorporated the symbol in their own way: cleverly, wittily and with affection. Edward Bawden used the device for the eye of a London pigeon, while for F.H.K. Henrion it became the mouth for a leaping figure. In other posters, the bar and circle could be seen at the scale of a cuff button, a hillside chalk drawing or the moon.

INVENTION AND ACADEMIC ACCLAIM

Reviewing the success of the bar-and-circle symbol in 1960, Professor of Art History Ernst Gombrich considered the ingenuity of its use while describing a phenomenon of looking at art. This is important in showing both the acceptance of transport advertising alongside the 'high' art of the academy, and as a critical appraisal from an unexpected quarter. Gombrich identified it as a 'stereotype, [an] identical symbol that we are made to recognise in different settings'.[18] He described how a widespread understanding of the symbol meant that by the mid-twentieth century it could be used in a 'frankly representational context' – as, for example, the frontal or profile view of the head of a cartoon figure or, at the other extreme, as a typographical element – without any loss of meaning. It was the potential for the symbol to seemingly be ambiguous in context that made it so specific, and strong. The pure beauty and utility of the London Transport brand mark was not lost on international observers either. New York's Museum of Modern Art, a world centre of avant-garde modernist thinking, included two London bus-stop signs in its 1954 exhibition 'Signs in the Street'.

London Transport's department of Public Relations and Publicity had a Copy and Ideas section, editing and writing advertisements, books, booklets and leaflets, and contributing to the art direction and graphics of all visual media across a network of 21,000 bus stops and signs, 1,250 passenger shelters and 7,250 poster sites. 1.45 million system maps were issued each year.[19] Publicity output took care of every aspect of the passenger's journey, from the scale of the city to the individual bus stop and travel ticket: 'Welcome to London', 'How to get there', 'Avoid rush hours', 'Always have the correct fare'. With Hutchison's sense of seizing every opportunity for promotion, the trading symbol featured in press advertisements and outdoor locations on rail and road networks, in vehicles and at stopping places. To restore travel after the bus workers' strike in 1958, the slogan 'Hop on a Bus' introduced a family of stick figures by the artist Lobban. Trips to the countryside around the capital came under the title 'Country Walks'. 'Shoppers' London' suggested a world of commerce to delight Londoners. When not 'speaking' to the public about travel, London Transport used publicity to recruit staff in the post-war period. Public service was becoming less attractive to young people, and the existing body of transport workers was getting older. Once more, the bar and circle was set to the task.

The 'How To Get There' campaign addressed the tourist and the Londoner, with a hardback guidebook, a visual explanation of London Transport, and the relevant system maps. The calligraphic rendering of the bar and circle was made by Edward Bawden.

The bulls-eye appeared in many forms in the printed output of the London Transport Publicity Office under the direction of Harold Hutchison.

Cartoon figures designed by Raymond Tooby featured in press advertisements and leaflets.

LONDON FROM A BUS TOP

The best way to see London is from the top of a bus—a moving grandstand from which to see in comfort the contrast of ancient buildings and busy streets. A leaflet describes many of the famous places of interest on particular bus routes and offers suggestions as to how you may spend a morning or an afternoon sightseeing for a shilling or so.

The leaflet is free from the Publicity Officer, London Transport, 55 Broadway, S.W.1.

MUSEUMS AND ART GALLERIES

London is full of interest on even the darkest afternoon. In the many museums and galleries are displays that will transport the visitor to other countries and other ages, ranging through the whole treasury of knowledge. This leaflet will help you to select the museum or gallery that best reflects your interests and tastes and will show you how to get there.

The leaflet is free from the Publicity Officer, London Transport, 55 Broadway, S.W.1.

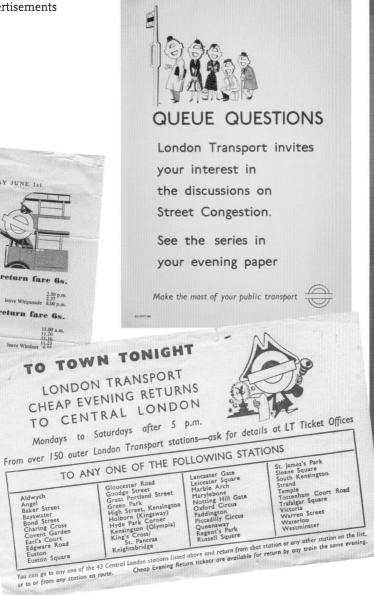

QUEUE QUESTIONS

London Transport invites your interest in the discussions on Street Congestion.

See the series in your evening paper

Make the most of your public transport

STARTING SUNDAY JUNE 1st

Sunday Bus Excursions

also on

Whit Monday and August Bank Holiday

Excursion No.

20 WHIPSNADE
Picking-up points
Mile End Station
Aldgate Bus Station

return fare 6s.

2.30 p.m.
2.37
leave Whipsnade 8.00 p.m.

25 WINDSOR
Picking-up points
Leyton, Ritz Cinema, High Road
Stratford, Empire Theatre
Mile End Station
Aldgate Bus Station

return fare 6s.

11.00 a.m.
11.10
11.16
11.23
leave Windsor 6.10

32 LONDON AIRPORT
Picking-up points
East Ham, 16/18 High Street South
Blackwall Tunnel, 202 East India
Poplar, 22/24 East India Dock Road

39 LONDON AIRPORT
Picking-up points
Mile End Station
Aldgate Bus Station

One child under 3 years of age, accompanied
occupying a seat, is carried free. Additional
children of 3 years and under 14 years of age

For list of booking agents see the reverse
to book, otherwise you can only trav

BY LONDON TRA

Area H

TO TOWN TONIGHT

LONDON TRANSPORT CHEAP EVENING RETURNS TO CENTRAL LONDON

Mondays to Saturdays after 5 p.m.

From over 150 outer London Transport stations—ask for details at LT Ticket Offices

TO ANY ONE OF THE FOLLOWING STATIONS

Aldwych	Gloucester Road	Lancaster Gate	St. James's Park
Angel	Goodge Street	Leicester Square	Sloane Square
Baker Street	Great Portland Street	Marble Arch	South Kensington
Bayswater	Green Park	Marylebone	Strand
Bond Street	High Street, Kensington	Notting Hill Gate	Temple
Charing Cross	Holborn (Kingsway)	Oxford Circus	Tottenham Court Road
Covent Garden	Hyde Park Corner	Paddington	Trafalgar Square
Earl's Court	Kensington (Olympia)	Piccadilly Circus	Victoria
Edgware Road	King's Cross/	Queensway	Warren Street
Euston	St. Pancras	Regent's Park	Waterloo
Euston Square	Knightsbridge	Russell Square	Westminster

You can go to any one of the 43 Central London stations listed above and return from that station or any other station on the list,
or to or from any station en route. Cheap Evening Return tickets are available for return by any train the same evening.

THE CHANGING OF THE GUARD

There are two ceremonies, one at the Horse Guards and the other either at Buckingham Palace or St. James's Palace. Together they provide London with a daily spectacle of unsurpassed brilliance and precision. A London Transport leaflet tells you when and where the ceremonies take place and describes the Brigade of Guards and the Household Cavalry, who provide the two guards.

The leaflet is free from the Publicity Officer, London Transport, 55 Broadway, S.W.1.

A successful move in communicating the advantages of public transport was the commissioning of illustrator/cartoonist Raymond Tooby, who provided many artworks for London Transport from 1949 to 1970. Tooby's humans and animals, with their bulls-eye heads, were both logotype and pictogram, succinctly engaging the viewer through surreal yet literal imagery. His work took the device to the limits of credibility and the apogee of testing its visual meaning. Many travel campaigns and events in London Transport history featured the work of Tooby and other artists.

A RETURN TO TRADITION

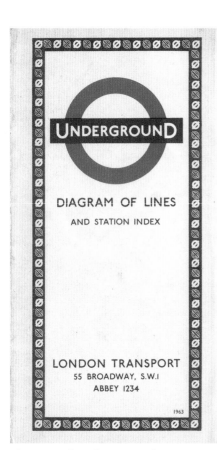

The original UndergrounD logotype returned to the system in 1956.

The middle part of Hutchison's period with London Transport brought him into direct contact with Sir John Elliot (1898–1988), an experienced professional railwayman whose career had been initiated by Lord Ashfield, head of the Underground Group. Elliot became intimately involved in the development of a modern 'house style' for the electric-train network in southern England, partly inspired by the example of the Underground. He was very aware of media relations through his family connection with the newspaper industry, his own work in publicity for England's Southern Railway and as Chairman of the nationalized British Railways system. When he became head of the London Transport Executive in 1953, Elliot remembered the example of railway branding set by Ashfield and launched a press appeal to determine how the bulls-eye had become the insignia of the organization.[20] The research results were inconclusive, but Elliot's close scrutiny extended to Harold Hutchison's changes to the symbol. Referring to the policy of naming the whole bus, rail and coach system 'London Transport' – which had been set in motion by Ashfield and his successor Lord Latham following Harold Hutchison's report – Elliot said, 'at my first [London Transport] Executive meeting I complained about the disappearance of the word from the Bull's Eye signs [sic] ... and 'UndergrounD' soon re-appeared all over the system'.[21] The old trading name was officially reintroduced in late 1956, displayed on bar-and-circle signs at stations and on line diagrams complete with the large initial and final letters first used in 1908. This was a definite assertion of tradition over modernity, and a clever way of establishing the unmistakable identity of the London railway system at a time when political emphasis was on nationalization and the homogenization of Britain's railways. The name was reproduced in the 1908 style until 1968, and has identified the system almost continually ever since.

For road-vehicle stopping places, the real innovation came out of cost-saving measures to reduce the number of signs in use. From 1949, stops served by both buses and coaches featured 'flag' signs split vertically into two colour-coded panels. Where one service mode was compulsorily required to stop and the other only by passenger request, half of the 'flag' had its colours reversed. The physical form of the sign was altered to produce a streamlined object with an aerofoil form, and a new post made to match. Commonly, these posts were of pre-cast concrete in a salmon-pink shade, producing colourful additions to the streetscape. This arrangement remained current practice for some 40 years.

London Transport was responsible for two important passenger-bus designs. Douglas Scott, working with London Transport's engineers, styled the RF coach in 1948–51 and the RM – Routemaster – bus in 1952–6. The RF featured a large, moulded bulls-eye symbol at the front end. The prototype Routemaster also carried this unmistakable motif, but for the first production models a more subtle plastic symbol was fitted above the radiator grille.

New roadside stop signs created in 1949 to combine indications for two different services in one flag.

Routemaster 1, the first prototype RM-type Routemaster bus, on its first day of service, 8 February 1956. The bus is photographed at the junction of Orchard Street and Oxford Street.

Staff who trained civilians during the Second World War were granted special badges to denote their status as instructors. Train, tram and trolleybus training personnel followed suit in 1948. This of course meant that every supervisory grade now wanted its own badge, leading to a system of different-coloured insignia and to some exotic designs being created as the organization grew in complexity. The four divisional colour schemes, continued until 1950, were: blue for central buses, red for trams and trolleybuses, yellow ochre for railways and green for country

Development of London Transport staff uniforms accelerated after 1945, and included the innovation of new insignia for senior grades. This station master at Piccadilly Circus is identified by the imperial laurel wreath within the ring of his gold-plated silver bar-and-circle cap badge.

Cap badges included the semi-official badge made for London Transport's own Military Band (TOP LEFT), and that of the four staff who controlled the express Green Line coach services through London's West End (BOTTOM RIGHT).

buses and coaches. Instructing and examining staff had turquoise-blue centres added to their badges; inspectors wore white centres, and the four men allocated to an office in Oxford Circus, London, to control express-coach operations wore orange centres to their green insignia. Artistic licence drifted into amateur heraldry, as groups and social clubs created their own unique designs (there was even a Junior Staff Club badge for children).

AFTER HUTCHISON

Bryce Beaumont had been the chief copywriter for London Transport posters since the late 1930s, writing much of the text for Hutchison's pair posters. After a period in which he left the organization to pursue a life in farming he was persuaded to return, succeeding Harold Hutchison as Publicity Officer in 1966. A somewhat different form of the symbol, rendered as fine outlines with or without lettering – which had been developed before the Second World War – was preferred by Beaumont. In this period, a rigorous separation of image and text allowed the outline bulls-eye to become the main identifying mark on posters until 1971. Budget reductions to the publicity programme also saw a decrease in the output of posters, but there were outstanding examples of clever bulls-eye interpretations from Tom Eckersley, Hans Unger and Abram Games in this period. The Victoria line, which opened in 1968, was marked by a special bulls-eye designed by Peter Roberson.

Creative poster artwork incorporating the bar and circle continued to be produced. LEFT: 'The City of London', poster by Abram Games, 1964; OPPOSITE, L–R: 'Art Today', poster by Hans Unger, 1966; 'Cut travelling time: Victoria Line', poster by Tom Eckersley, 1969.

ART TODAY The Tate, re-hung with taste and logic, offers the academically approved, the Whitechapel the young and middle-generation painters. The Greater London Council sets contemporary British sculpture against the simpler pleasures of Battersea Park. Complete your survey with the commercial galleries of deepest Mayfair and Chelsea, and the avant-garde extremes. For all these new frontiers, the explorer's kit is simple—an open mind, Underground and bus maps, and a sense of humour. For The Tate Gallery: Underground or bus to Westminster, then bus 77B. For The Whitechapel Art Gallery: Underground to Aldgate East. For Battersea Park: Underground to Sloane Square, then by bus 137.

By 1971, the London Transport system had a bulls-eye for almost every purpose and every person: too many, perhaps. The main-line British Railways had undergone a total rebranding programme at the hands of Design Research Unit, completed in 1965. Pursuing a vision that the minimum of means would have the maximum impact, and using a cool, crisp association of type, logo and colour palette in the style of Swiss typography, the British Rail that emerged from this programme was proclaimed internationally as an example of good modern transport design.[22] As we will see in the next chapter, it would now be London's turn.

The special version of the bulls-eye designed by Peter Roberson for the Victoria line.

BRAVE NEW LONDON

Leaflet promoting modern architectural achievements such as office blocks, housing estates and schools across the capital, published 1960. This outline form of the bar and circle saw increased use in the period 1966–71.

5

ECONOMY AND MONOPOLY

By this point in the story of the London Transport bar and circle it will be evident that, throughout its life, the symbol has been subject to alternating and competing programmes of ornamentation and plainness. In this chapter, we begin with a return to the unadorned form of the brand.

Hans Schleger's work to revise the trading mark in the mid-1930s had been in the vanguard of modern design. He demonstrated that, as the symbol was so well known to the public, it was understood as representative of a complex of transport networks, from a single sign to an entire railway system. It also stood for reliability in service, and as an authoritative 'voice' communicating with the public. Harold Hutchison and his successor as London Transport Publicity Officer, Bryce Beaumont, maintained the bar and circle in parallel states. One was entirely at the discretion of the artist or designer and might be playful or severe; the other conformed to a standard solid- or outline-silhouette typographical pattern. As plans came together for the Victoria line in the early 1960s, London Transport decided that it needed an external design practice to give advice on the project. The outcome of this consultancy would be a drastic rationalization of the trading mark and its associated corporate identity.

Misha Black and Milner Gray had been active in the London and international design community since the 1930s. In 1929 Gray had been a founder member of the Society of Industrial Artists (SIA), later called the Society of Industrial Artists and Designers (SIAD). Promoting the profession and the education of industrial artists – not then called designers – the society brought together 'fine' artists and industrial artists, much as Frank Pick did for the Underground, and others were doing for Shell Oil and the General Post Office.[1] Industrial Design Partnership was founded by Gray and Black in 1935 in order to work on graphic design, industrial design and architectural projects; it was dissolved in 1940 because of war commitments. However, it was not long before they came together again formally, in the team of associate designers called Design Research Unit (DRU).[2] The SIA London group, formed after the Second World War, included Milner Gray and Misha Black. Black was one of five members of the Design Group for the 1951 Festival of Britain, directing DRU's work there. Other members of DRU included the Director, Herbert Read; architects Sadie Speight and Frederick Gibberd; structural engineer Felix Samuely; and designers George Williams (later British Railways' Director of Industrial Design) and Norbert Dutton, who wrote one of the first detailed appraisals of London Transport design in 1946.[3]

DRU specialized in all-inclusive architecture, interior, graphic and product design projects, creating comprehensive corporate-design programmes. It acted as consultant to large public organizations, including the British Overseas Airways Corporation, Westminster City Council, the General Post Office and the British Airports Authority, and for private companies (British Petroleum, Imperial Chemical Industries, Watney Mann Brewery). One major accomplishment of DRU was the British Rail corporate identity programme of 1956–66 – a rebranding project aimed at uniting five disparate regional transport groups, each claiming its own identity carried over from the early twentieth century. All parts of the national rail network were progressively updated, new signs, publicity and vehicle liveries erasing the old.

As the unit was embarking on the core of British Rail's brand identity in 1963–4, London Transport recruited Misha Black to be its consultant for trains, stations, signs and industrial design on the forthcoming Victoria line project. Black joined a design panel composed of the London Transport Chairman, the Chief Architect, and Publicity Officer Harold Hutchison. Black designed for the long term: his projects for British Rail and London Transport combined beauty and robustness with an apparent simplicity, which has preserved their visual integrity and functionality long after contemporary designs have become redundant or old-fashioned. He also aimed for high standards of aesthetic purity and efficiency of means, maintaining throughout the affluent 1950s and early 1960s a rigour which had been imposed when design – and designers – were vital tools in the necessary economy of fighting the Second World War.

After the Victoria line project, DRU worked on the London Transport corporate identity. The client was now a new executive under the financial control of the Greater London Council (GLC). The country-bus and coach network had been transferred out of the business in 1970. DRU began with the *Design Survey Report* of 1971, and Misha Black made his first recommendations in January 1972. Consultancy continued for some years in tandem with the design of the Fleet line between Charing Cross and Baker Street, which opened as the Jubilee line in 1979.

Unlike Hans Schleger, who had used imaginative variety in his stripping down of the bulls-eye device in the mid-1930s, DRU brought a considerable austerity to the programme. Picking up on the proliferation of patriotic symbols in 'pop' tourist goods during the late 1960s, Misha Black said soberly that the historical use of the London Transport symbol 'in a variety of forms, inconsistencies of shape, repetitively as borders to printed material and with humorous connotations, is as inappropriate as a girl's Union Jack printed [under]pants'.[4] Black contended that the bar and circle, redrawn and named 'the roundel', would wholly embody the organization *London Transport*. It did not need lettering across the symbol: 'Publicity should be mobilized to give it the authority of the Queen's Head on a stamp which makes the name of the country redundant.' The roundel was to be displayed in a severely restricted colour palette of red, white or black only, whatever its application. The Design Panel agreed that new proportions for the roundel 'would be adopted throughout London Transport for all future new and replacement signs, publicity, stationery, etc'. All other versions of the symbol were to be prohibited.

Harold Hutchison had discovered in the late 1940s, when he tried to abandon the word *Underground*, that the organization protected the success of its symbol with vigour. Reviewing the traditional red, white and

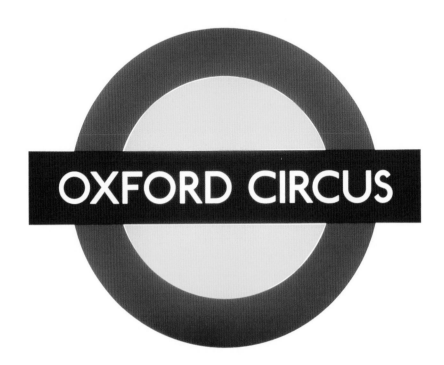

ABOVE: Artworks prepared to show the new London Transport roundel as a station nameboard, with and without the yellow infills proposed by Design Research Unit to make the signs more distinctive.

LEFT: Mocked-up nameboard with the yellow infills in combination with a blue bar, after railway staff objected to the threatened loss of their established identifying symbol.

For new station name friezes, the curious proposal was made that, at platforms served by more than one line, the darker line colour would form a border and be the colour of the roundel and lettering, on a band of the lighter line colour: e.g. District line green on Circle line yellow, Metropolitan line purple on Circle line yellow, Metropolitan line purple on District line green. Other station name friezes would be unchanged.

blue colour scheme of London Transport, DRU felt that blue reduced the bright effect of the red. How, then, to address the tricky issue of station nameboards, a question which seems to have been missed by Design Research Unit until late in the project? As had happened in 1906–8, paper signs were made for evaluation in situ on station platforms. The all-red roundel and the blue-and-red symbol were installed at Sloane Square on opposite platforms.[5] Yellow was added to the semicircular counters of one nameboard to see if the colour gave additional brightness. Neither operator nor public favoured the changes. One symbol fixed outside an Underground station so perturbed the London Transport Chairman that it and its fellows had to be removed immediately. If the forces of tradition and common sense were not enough, there was insufficient budget to implement the DRU proposals across the system. As a compromise to encompass the presence of older signs on the railway system, a second bar-and-circle symbol was defined as the 'bulls-eye', drawn in the new roundel proportions, coloured blue and red.[6]

Publicity Officer Bryce Beaumont retired in 1975, to be succeeded by Michael F. Levey. In-house graphic designer Tim Demuth was tasked with making the Design Research Unit proposals workable in everyday use. He redesigned the bus-stop flag signs and, importantly, redrafted the roundel once more to fit a typographical grid.[7] The entire project was collected together in the London Transport Design Manual of 1977.

The corporate identity was summarized as follows: 'The London Transport symbol is the Roundel. When representing London Transport it is to appear in Bus Red or white out of 'Bus Red' (Central line red). There should be no wording on the roundel and no adaptation or freehand representation of the roundel. The logotype is the Roundel with wording in Edward Johnston's typeface alongside giving the name London Transport, Underground or Buses.'

Buses would carry the plain white Roundel on red paintwork.

Exterior signs were simplified. This one combines the London Transport roundel with the British Rail double arrow, also the result of a DRU corporate identity programme.

London Buses

MAP AND LIST OF ROUTES

ISSUED FREE

LONDON TRANSPORT

55 BROADWAY, S.W.1
01-222 1234

Informazione Turistica

COMPRESO PIANTE
METROPOLITANA
ED AUTOBUS

LONDON TRANSPORT

55 BROADWAY, S.W.1
01-222 1234

ITALIAN 1972

Informations Touristiques

AVEC PLANS
DU MÉTRO
ET DES AUTOBUS

LONDON TRANSPORT

55 BROADWAY, S.W.1
01-222 1234

FRENCH 1972

Touristen-Informationen

EINSCHLIESSLICH
U·BAHN·
UND BUSPLÄNEN

LONDON TRANSPORT

55 BROADWAY, S.W.1
01-222 1234

GERMAN 1972

VANDALISM

on the
P2 bus route

AN IMPORTA
MESSAGE F
LONDO
TRANSP

LONDON TRANSPORT

Bargain Tickets

ON BUSES AND THE UNDERGROUND

GO-AS-YOU-PLEASE TICKETS
(4-DAY, 7-DAY, MONTHLY AND ANNUAL)
RED BUS SEASONS
(MONTHLY AND ANNUAL)
RED BUS ROVERS
(DAILY)
UNDERGROUND CHEAP DAY RETURNS
(DAILY)
UNDERGROUND SEASON TICKETS

Victoria Line TIMES AND FARES

Autumn 1972

The changes were
reflected in the austere
design of folder maps
and publicity.

Even at the time of the *Design Manual*, creative invention was testing the monolithic identity of the organization. The human desire to embellish and decorate could not be suppressed, and the roundel found its way into various logos for special services and commemorative events. The 150th anniversary of the London omnibus in 1979 prompted a highly decorative bar and circle based on the livery of the original vehicle, while a new Underground line, initially named the Fleet, and retitled the Jubilee, had its own crown-with-roundel device. Operational restructuring of the London Buses network in 1979 led to vehicles and publicity being identified with eight different district names and logotypes. In architectural settings, designers made great play of the bar-and-circle shape in doors, windows and decorative brickwork. The organization began to retail its own souvenir products at this time, again exploiting the value of the trading symbol beyond the limits of the corporate identity declared in 1972.

Design Research Unit's recommendations were only ever partly implemented, since economic constraints came to bear on the business and because the unit argued against the established identity. In retrospect the project was ambitious but insensitive, lacking understanding of how London itself perceived the symbol with which it travelled every day. With a clear sense that moves to unify the visual cohesion of London Transport were facing tests from within, we now move to the next chapter, in which external political forces would act to formally divide the organization.

ABOVE: Embellishment of the roundel was occasionally still permitted for purposes of publicity, celebration or commemoration. William Fenton used the wreath of flowers from George Shillibeer's original omnibus to mark 150 years of London's buses in 1979.

LEFT: The symbol was incorporated into many architectural features, as shown by these door handles at Hatton Cross station.

We're here to help

⊖ Buses, Underground, Green Line Coaches
Ring 01-222 1234 day or night or call at any
London Transport Information Centre

⇌ British Rail, ring
01-283 7171 (Fenchurch Street, Liverpool Street)
01-387 3355 (Moorgate, King's Cross)
01-387 7070 (Midland Region)
01-262 6767 (Western Region)
01-925 5100 (Southern Region) or call at the
Travel Centre Lower Regent Street W1

Artwork for a travel information
poster proposed by Tom
Eckersley in 1984.

6

REDEFINING THE IDENTITY

DESIGN EVERYWHERE

Britain became aware of design as a cultural practice as the 1970s ended. Punk rock, fashion and graphics placed design overtly in the context of the everyday. 'Industrial artists' were now 'industrial designers', and industrial designers had names and personalities. 'Commercial artists' had long-since become 'graphic designers', and these too came into public familiarity, as typographers, magazine art directors, packaging specialists and album-cover artists crafted visuals for our consumption. Cultural commentators and museums brought the public into contact with international design and its authors. Museum shops began to sell 'design'. Design was more clearly understood as an important tool in the process of shaping the man-made world. Soon, it was an essential component of living, inextricable with lifestyle – a necessity. Alongside this, 'corporate identity' had transformed into 'brand'. Of course, this had long been the message from individuals like Frank Pick and agencies such as Design Research Unit.

The effect on London Transport of this cultural shift was evident from the mid-1980s, when money was released for improvement works to facilities in central London in order to facelift a system which seemed stuck in time, tired and dirty. Underground stations benefited from a significant investment programme, which brought together artists and architects for ostentatious projects. These, in turn, would be surpassed by the technical and spatial excellence of the Jubilee line extension, opened in 1999. Under Head of Design Jeremy Rewse-Davies and Graphic Design, Environmental Design and Product Design Managers Corynne Bredin, Christopher Nell and Innes Ferguson, there was a marked revival in design at London Transport. Their approach was to combine the best strands of design practice, proven by London Transport's extensive heritage, and to invite modern solutions where appropriate. New design standards were codified in a series of guideline documents covering

AFTER 50 YEARS, IS THIS THE END OF THE LINE?

LONDON TRANSPORT

The Transport Bill means higher fares and fewer services.
Kill the Bill. Phone 633 4400

GLC
Working for London

21 MARCH

London Transport
100% Increases*
from
Westminster

Is this fair on London?

KEEP FARES FAIR

ACT NOW! Sign the petitions, write to the press, tell your MP.

Publicity for the 'Fares Fair' campaign of 1981–2.

topics such as recommended colours for station structures, use of the organization's corporate identity, and protection of its intellectual property – the brand itself. London Transport Museum Retail Manager Michael Walton worked in partnership with Jeremy Rewse-Davies to commission poster artworks for the Underground. Every aspect of London Underground was considered, and design restored to a coordinated ubiquity. The roundel trading symbol would subtly identify many aspects of this aesthetic renaissance.

DIVIDE AND SELL

During the 1970s, London Transport maintained a course of operating road and rail services across the metropolis and suburbs, much as it had done since the Second World War. It introduced conductor-less buses and guard-less trains in order to reduce costs, and worked to reshape the bus network for further economy in the face of increased road-traffic congestion and changed patterns of use. Ultimately, it remained a civil service department of the then Labour-party-controlled Greater London Council (GLC). With the election of a Conservative government in 1979, the same year that it celebrated 150 years since George Shillibeer had brought omnibus services to the city, London Transport found itself in an explicitly political context. The GLC wanted to establish a certain standpoint in the face of the Tory administration. With control of

London's travel infrastructure, it had a powerful means of communicating its message.

The Fares Fair campaign of 1981–2 for subsidized travel costs was a GLC strategy to restore use of public transport. It became the subject of a legal battle initiated by a Tory-controlled borough council, and the strategy was overturned. Quickly the situation polarized, so that the national administration moved to dismantle London's governing body. London Transport commemorated 50 years of activity in 1983, and 60 years in 1993. In 1984, enabled by the Transport Act of that year, London Transport services were moved from the GLC to direct state control through a new body called London Regional Transport (LRT). The council was abolished two years later. LRT retained the trading name *London Transport* but set about meeting its legal obligation to separate the bus and rail parts of the business for eventual privatization. London Buses Limited and London Underground Limited were formed in 1985.

The all-red roundel, which had identified London Transport for some 12 years, clearly could not represent two de-merging companies. Several design practices were brought in for a rebranding exercise, now using corporate identity to split up the businesses rather than unite them. London Regional Transport commissioned its own symbol, an anonymous logotype which effectively subdued the parent organization in favour of its subsidiaries. It was not successful, and lasted but a few years. International brand consultants Wolff Olins advised on the design of 'one Roundel for the idea of London Transport; a system of Roundels to link and separate the transport operating businesses from the other businesses; a way of separating the two major transport businesses'.[1] In a repeat of not so distant history, Wolff Olins proposed one colour (blue) for roundels for both the railway and bus businesses. London Underground insisted on retaining the historic red-and-blue symbol. In light of its heritage, London Buses wanted the blue-and-red logo too. To maintain distinction of services in advance of the bus network being further broken up for privatization, another colour scheme had to be found. After experiments with green, pink, turquoise and white, the consultants proposed a roundel with a yellow bar.[2] This was carried on vehicles from mid-1987 until the bus-operating units were sold off to private companies in 1994–5. To serve the regenerated dockland area in east London, a light-railway network opened in 1987. For a brief period it was operated by London Regional Transport, and so, after experimenting with a wavy river-like bar, Wolff Olins provided a roundel with a pale blue name label.[3]

The proposed and final logos of the Docklands Light Railway.

Some of Wolff Olin's experiments with the London Buses logo, before settling on the yellow bar.

A NEW IMAGE FOR THE RAILWAYS

London Underground now looked to its estate. There was much to do, with design and branding central to the endeavour. On the railway system, the corporate identity was represented by many different forms of bulls-eye and roundel signs, the result of successive policy and design changes which had never been fully implemented. Chris Ludlow, partner in design consultant Henrion, Ludlow & Schmidt, takes up the story:

Corporate identity – and London Underground
The benefits of a strong corporate identity are usually extolled in a competitive situation, where the 'positioning' of an organization, or a brand, is defined in terms of differences from the competition. What, therefore, has corporate identity to do with a service provider in an apparently non-competitive situation?

Starting with its 'positioning', we could say that a public transport system should be perceived as being open, efficient and responsive. Although a small element of formal promotional communication is carried out by London Underground, the main channels for communication of its corporate identity are through physical assets, staff presentation and behaviour, and passenger information. The physical assets, including stations and trains, are long-term investments which are not easily changed in the short term. Staff presentation and behaviour are 'soft' aspects which are not easy to control. Passenger information is partly fixed (signs) and partly responsive to day-to-day requirements (announcements, screens, notices). It is very clear that, for an urban transport system, the establishment of a solid and positive corporate identity is above all a very long-term matter, involving both intangible and tangible factors.

During the 1980s, it was more usual to consider corporate identity as simply the outward manifestation of an organization, but Henrion, Ludlow & Schmidt had always rejected this concept as superficial and, moreover, ultimately ineffective. The inward-facing aspects of a strong corporate identity are now generally recognized. Pride in working for an organization is of course reinforced when the outward impression is positive. But, in addition, when employees are involved in the corporate identity process, they are more likely to implement that identity enthusiastically and correctly, which leads to a virtuous circle of buy-in. When employees face the public, they are also more likely to present themselves in an appropriate manner, both visually and through their behaviour. Indeed, standards of personal presentation for London Underground staff were eventually produced, involving staff and union consultation.

The establishment of a coordinated sign system, starting in 1984, with internal systems for planning and implementation and comprehensive guidelines, was a precursor for the production of a comprehensive set of standards for all visual manifestations. Even though the range and complexity of the standards was exceptional, they could be considered as a normal approach to a conventional corporate identity project (which lasted for nearly 15 years!). However, the most radical aspect was the relationship of corporate identity standards to the culture and procedures of London Underground.

Remember that the Kings Cross fire of November 1987 occurred during the time that the sign system was being designed, and that the competence of the Underground's management was being widely questioned. The system was also creaking, deprived of essential investment in infrastructure and rolling stock. Staff reorganizations were to lead to widespread discontent and demoralization. It was against this background that standards for all aspects of the Underground's management, systems, installations and equipment were identified and implemented. Corporate identity standards provided a template for many others, and contributed a highly visible example of professionalism and consistency. This affected the internal culture and, eventually, the look of the entire system. The Underground of 2012 is very different from the Underground of 1984.

BACK TO THE BAR AND CIRCLE

London Regional Transport recognized that its own device meant little to the public; it restored the red roundel created by Design Research Unit in 1972. From 1990, this symbol was brought back into prominence and close association with the trading name *London Transport* to represent rail and road in joint publicity, with the separate modal roundels identifying individual services. David Pocknell prepared new corporate guidelines to reunite the different elements of the system. At the same time, a management structure for bus operation in London was created, with a subtly altered title: London's Buses. This became London Transport Buses in 1994, marked by a white roundel on a red square. The first road-borne rail service since 1952 opened as the Croydon Tramlink in 2000. It received a green version of the London Transport Buses mark. London River Services, a network of licensed boat operators, carried a blue version of the symbol.

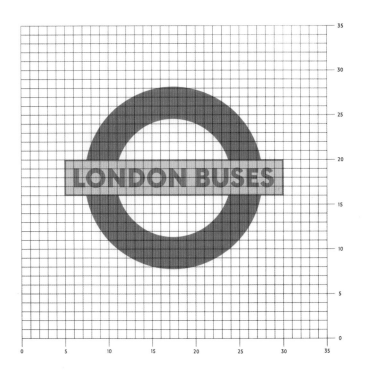

The Buses roundel is a version of the London Transport roundel. It differs by being reproduced in red and yellow, the house colours of London Buses Limited, and by having the words 'London Buses' in the yellow horizontal bar.

For print applications, the roundel must always be reproduced photographically from original negatives such as those contained in the pocket at the back of this booklet. No attempt should be made to typeset the words 'London Buses' or render them by any other means, whatever the circumstances.

When using non-opaque colours make certain the words 'London Buses' are reversed out of the yellow bar first so that the lettering prints red not orange.

The basic proportions of this roundel are not correct, so it cannot have been reproduced photographically from the correct source.

Here, the lettering has been typeset with the wrong spacing. Photographic reproduction from the correct source would eliminate this problem.

For checking purposes and for large-scale planning or construction of the basic outline, a construction grid is indicated on this page. The lettering must not be reproduced using this grid.

In no circumstances is the roundel to be reproportioned or modified in any way.

This poor reproduction could be caused by a number of things and is not acceptable. Direct photographic reproduction from the correct source would eliminate such problems.

3

2

Guidelines for the use of the final London Buses roundel, which was carried on vehicles from 1987 until 1994–5.

How was this family of marks used? Printed material featured the coloured symbols of the modes relevant to the publicity content. Posters initially followed a standard layout, with the roundel shown independently of the image. Publicity leaflets gave designers some freedom to express the roundel pictorially for themes such as Easter and Christmas.

The rail network experienced a comprehensive revision of signs in accordance with Henrion, Ludlow & Schmidt's guidelines, producing a clear and consistent system of identification elements; this has since been adopted as the model for London Buses infrastructure and other modes operated by Transport for London. Those of historical interest were put into the care of the London Transport Museum, and surplus items sold by auction through salerooms and the *London Transport Museum Friends* magazine. This project continues in 2013. Station exteriors received new signs, designed by Derek Hodgson Associates, Edinburgh. Design of

Leaflets showing the three new roundels for buses, tram and river services, alongside the first Transport for London brand mark in 2000.

station environments for the Jubilee line extension (1999) included a range of three-dimensional station nameboards. For London Underground Anne Tyrrell Design created new staff uniforms based on a colour scheme of blue and silver/grey. London Buses carried the yellow-and-red roundel until the fleet was privatized. There then followed a range of logos and brands of varying quality, selected by the operators. Bus-stopping places were subject to a London-wide programme of modernization, using an innovative and award-winning modular post-and-sign system by Jedco Product Designers.[4]

Having come through a period of upheaval and change, the London public transport system was now comprehensively improved and coherently identified: it was time for change, again.

Three-dimensional station nameboards designed for the 1999 Jubilee line extension.

Simply Fashion by Tube and bus

Image commissioned by London Transport from Trickett & Webb (homage to Man Ray).
This poster is available from the London Transport Museum, Covent Garden Piazza.

Look out for the special leaflet, produced in conjunction with Time Out magazine, coming through your door or pick one up from Underground stations and selected newsagents, or visit us at www.londontransport.co.uk

The roundel appears in various forms on posters, leaflets and postcards from the 1990s to the 2010s. Despite rigorous control of the corporate image in recent years, London's transport administration has continued to display imaginative uses of the roundel.

LEFT: 'Simply fashion by Tube and bus', poster by Trickett and Webb, 1999, adapting Man Ray's original Underground poster of 1938 (see p. 61).

OPPOSITE: 'In the past year, almost half our stations have had a face lift', poster, 1993.

**In the past year,
almost half our stations have had a face lift.**

Over the past twelve months we've been busy giving a bright, fresh look to
119 of our 248 stations. They've been repainted and many have been given new wall and floor tiles.
All have had new easy to read signing installed. We'd like to do more, and we will
when funds are available. It's all part of our aim to give you a brighter, smarter Underground.

You can't beat the Tube.

Transport for London

Fly across the Thames

A new connection between the O2 and ExCeL

The Emirates Air Line
London's first cable car

MAYOR OF LONDON

Emirates AIR·LINE

The roundel entered an exciting new phase of use as it took to the air for the cross-river cable-car link. Here it both branded a non-terrestrial transport mode for the first time, and was combined in a single logotype with the branding of a commercial organization.

7

MILLENNIAL MOVES

EVERYTHING HAS ITS MARK

By the end of the twentieth century the philosophy of total design, which had been practised by London Transport since the 1920s, was established as a theoretical and practical concept for organizing business and retailing product. Semiological theories work to decode and explain systems of signs and meanings. Organizations form their staff and strategies around brands, whether they are charities, holiday providers, nightclub owners, or food or service companies. Commerce uses the pseudo-science of signs, through labelling of clothes and objects, to construct brands with sophisticated and desirable qualities that are used to market goods.

To mark the comprehensive renewal of London Underground's infrastructure, a series of 'Upgrade' roundels have been displayed across the network on publicity and at building locations.

Multiplicities of things around us have a 'look', and a brand; often the two qualities are interlinked. Brands jump international borders, named sportswear garments become uniforms. 'Brand extension' has emerged as a marketing and design practice, meaning that companies extend their logos to products other than those for which they have been traditionally known. Now, Ferrari and Mini cars have clothing stores, fashion designer Paul Smith styles cars, chefs create cooking utensils, and celebrities curate museum exhibitions. Entire cities are represented by single marks; conversely, there are niche brands and exclusive products to stimulate greater craving for ownership. Brands sell.

These trends and innovations have affected the transport systems in London in various ways. In this chapter, we look at how brand extension has been implemented to organize several modes of travel in the city. In subsequent chapters, we consider how *London Transport* has been retailed by the organization as a souvenir and lifestyle brand, and how the bar and circle has been appropriated and subverted by agencies outside the official corporate body.

EXTENDING THE BRAND

The pervasive strength of the bar and circle has been reaffirmed in recent years. Transport for London (TfL) came into being on 3 July 2000 as the public-service operating subsidiary of the Greater London Authority (GLA). Once again, the network was under the direct control of London's administrative body. The creation of the GLA initially led to speculation about both the extension of the roundel into other transport services, and its abolition. In fact it heralded a period of reunification, with TfL positioned as the overall controller of transport networks in the capital. Soon coordination of the different modes was gathered closer to the centre once more, Transport for London demonstrating how brand extension can be applied to an apparently monolithic and utilitarian identity, to generate a whole family of distinct yet related symbols.

Transport for London administers several modes. Victoria Coach Station has been owned by London Transport since 1988. London Tramlink in Croydon (fully operational since 2000) is delivered by a leasing arrangement. The Rail Services Division of TfL included Docklands Light Railway (DLR) from 2001, with a considerably extended system developed through east and south-east London. London Underground Limited came under TfL management in 2003. London Overground – 'the new orbital rail

OPPOSITE: Different versions of the roundel will continue to appear as the networks are extended to further modes of transport.

PMS 072c/072u

PMS 072c/072u

PMS Warm Red c/u

PMS Warm Red c/u

PMS 072c/072u
PMS Warm Red c/u

PMS 072c/072u

PMS Warm Red c/u

PMS Warm Red c/u

PMS 072c/072u
PMS 326c/326u

PMS 326c/326u

PMS 072c/072u
PMS 368c/368u

PMS 368c/368u

PMS 072c/072u
PMS 2715c/2715u

PMS 2715c/2715u

PMS 072c/072u
PMS 130c/130u

PMS 130c/130u

PMS 072c/072u
PMS 219c/219u

PMS 219c/219u

PMS 072c/072u
PMS 299c/299u

PMS 299c/299u

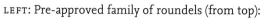

LEFT: Pre-approved family of roundels (from top):

Transport for London (and London Transport Museum)	all blue or all red
London Underground	blue bar/red ring or all blue
Buses	all red
Light Rail	blue bar/turquoise ring or all turquoise
Trams	blue bar/green ring or all green
Taxis	blue bar/lilac ring or all lilac
Coaches (and Victoria Coach Station from 2007)	blue bar/light orange ring or all light orange
Street Management	blue bar/fuschia ring or all fuschia
Boats	blue bar/light blue ring or all light blue

network for London' – launched in 2007 and linked fragments of several former rail routes in west, north, north-west, east and south London into an extensive urban system during 2010–11. DLR is operated by a licensee and London Overground is managed by a consortium. The latter company forms part of the national rail network. London River Services, part of TfL, works with many boat companies on the Thames and provides much of the infrastructure.[1] Dial a Ride supports those who have difficulty accessing standard services. Already we can see that the roundel, which identifies all these modes, works beyond its original limits to create the sense of a single authoritative entity from diverse service-provision arrangements. Beyond conventionally understood public transport modes, the TfL remit now incorporates 'black' taxi cabs and private-hire mini cabs, and the control of street and highway projects. The Barclays [Bank] Cycle Hire Scheme commenced in July 2010 and has since grown substantially across inner London; sensibly, the Cycle Hire roundel is a blue close to Barclays' own brand identity. The Emirates Air Line cable car, sponsored by the international flight operator, opened on 28 June 2012 as the latest service to be branded with a roundel. This last mode is promoted in contemporary parlance as 'The Experience', and presented by an assembly of companies, the 'front of house team' being provided by Continuum, one of the UK's largest visitor-attractions groups.

London Transport's Design Management team had set a standard for enshrining corporate-identity practice in the 1990s. Transport for London produces Design Standards for all its modes, accounting for every likely application.[2] The family of roundels has changed in recent years to allow new operations to be branded. At the head of the family is the Transport for London roundel, reproduced entirely in red, blue, black or white according to context. This is seen on many posters and publicity items, and marks the Oyster plastic smartcard, London's electronic ticket. There then follow several service marks, shown opposite in their provisional form. Modal roundels appear on vehicles, publicity and signs. Personnel in contact with the public are identified by name badges with an appropriately coloured roundel, while other items of clothing may carry unlettered symbols: that for London Underground is usually silver, and for London Buses is white.

How the Crossrail stations, due to open from late 2018, will be signed is yet to be confirmed. In July 2012, the Mayor of London made a proposal to the Department for Transport that would see TfL managing suburban rail services across the metropolis. The implications for passengers are greater consistency in services, ticketing and station environments as

A special logo marks the 150th anniversary of London Underground in 2013.

Publicity providing travel advice during the 2012 Olympic and Paralympic Games displayed the roundel alongside the London 2012 logo.

several private rail operators are unified. Ideas for the branding of this system are not yet public, but TfL does have a 'Rail' modal roundel in reserve at the time of writing. The logo designed to mark the occasion of London Underground's 150th anniversary in 2013 comprises the number 150 in New Johnston type, with the zero formed by the blue and red Underground roundel.

In 2012 London hosted the Olympic and Paralympic Games for the third time in the city's history, raising key issues related to branding and transport. London 2012's own prominent brand, vision and logo, developed by consultancy Wolff Olins (authors of the 1985–6 London Buses roundel) and launched in 2007, was rigorously protected and vigorously promoted by the Games' organizers.[3] With strong emphasis placed on the integration of public transport into the events, it was necessary to form an association between two prominent symbols: the roundel and the London 2012 logo. The Transport for London identity – manifested by the New Johnston typeface – was used across all aspects of the 2012 Games, from signage through to maps. In providing directional signs around the transport networks, the Games' brand was seen in general proximity to the roundel, especially on London Underground signs and platforms. A special project called 'Get Ahead of the Games' was developed by 'Transport for London on behalf of the Olympic Delivery Authority, London 2012, the Department for Transport, the Highways Agency, National Rail and the Mayor of London'.[4] The initiative offered several levels of information about moving around the city during the Games, while a series of posters, press advertisements and leaflets displayed the roundel and the London 2012 logo in tandem.

London 2012 'Gold' poster, displayed across the network to celebrate Team GB's success. 'Silver' and 'Bronze' versions were also produced.

Joëlle Tuerlinckx, 'Untitled'.

8

ART ON THE UNDERGROUND

Art on the Underground (AotU) grew out of the Platform for Art initiative to restore a high level of artistic quality to the environment of the London Underground system.[1] Since 2000, many works have been created through the initiative, and are recorded in the book *Platform for Art: Art on the Underground* (2007). The roundel occurs in various contexts in AotU projects; one example is artist David Batchelor's 'Ten silhouettes' installation at Gloucester Road station in 2005, which made use of reclaimed station nameboard signs for some of its pieces.[2]

Tamsin Dillon, Head of Art on the Underground, was invited to give a commentary on *100 Years, 100 Artists, 100 Works of Art*,[3] the most significant AotU project to feature the roundel:

In 2008, Art on the Underground commissioned one hundred new works of art to mark the centenary of the Roundel. One hundred international

'World Class Art for a World Class Tube'

'Ten silhouettes', installation by David Batchelor at Gloucester Road station, 2005, for the Art on the Underground scheme.

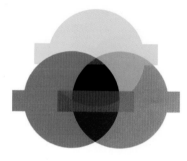

Leaflet featuring the Art on the
Underground project to celebrate
100 years of the roundel in 2008.

artists at various stages in their career, from recent graduates to individuals with worldwide reputations, were invited to make a new artwork inspired by the symbol: one of the world's most recognized brands. Their responses – imaginative and playful, bold and irreverent – reinterpret, reinvent and celebrate an iconic emblem of the city of London. The intention behind the project was to present a contemporary vision of the Tube, and to build on the long tradition of artists who have worked under the patronage of London Underground.

The project put a spotlight on the Roundel in its centenary year, and on the Art on the Underground programme as a whole. An exhibition of the original contributions was held in an east London gallery, and an auction was staged to sell one of a limited edition of two prints of each work. The other prints remain as a collection and a resource that continues to be reproduced for special posters all over the Underground.

This chapter presents a selection of images from the *100 Years, 100 Artists, 100 Works of Art* project.

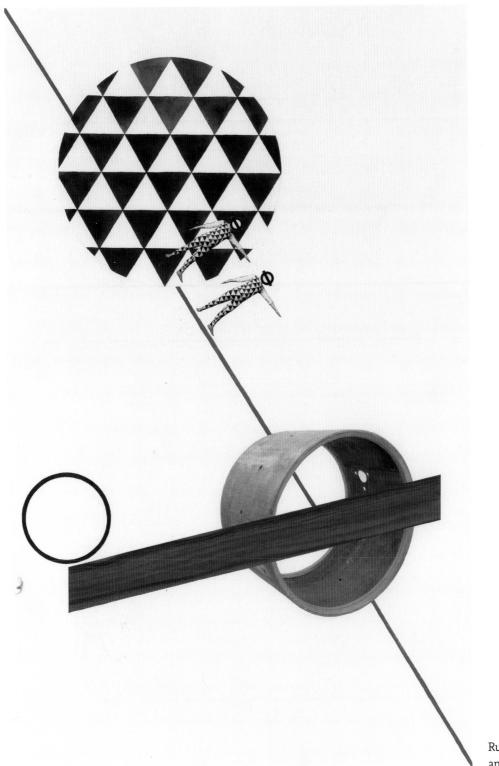

Ruth Proctor, 'Every One an Island'.

OPPOSITE: Paul Noble, 'O I O'.

ABOVE, L–R: Scott King, 'Untitled';
Olivia Plender, 'A desire to have the
best of both worlds'.

UNDERGROUND

MOVEMENTS MAKE THE CITY CHANGE

Eline McGeorge, 'Movements make the city change'.

Around stretches the vast expanse of the world

Simon and Tom Bloor,
'Around stretches the vast
expanse of the world'.

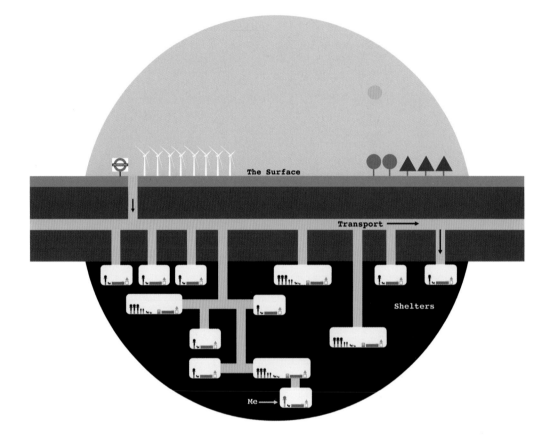

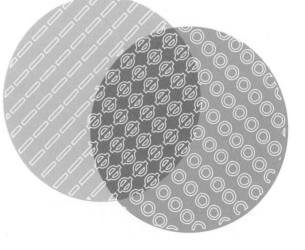

OPPOSITE: Charlie Tweed,
'It's time to go below'.

ABOVE, L–R: Marta Marcé,
'Circulating'; Henry Coleman,
'Poster design (Venn Roundel)'.

9

TAKE LONDON HOME WITH YOU

The number 88 bus from Clapham Common to Camden Town passes through many important tourist spots in London: Westminster, Whitehall, Trafalgar Square, Piccadilly Circus, Oxford Circus and Camden Market. This south–north route is a marvellous way to see London as it should be seen – from the top deck of a bus – and a trip on it will reveal the preponderance of gift and souvenir shops selling merchandise and mementos of the city. An important element of this souvenir industry is items branded with the bar-and-circle symbol, usually in blue and red. This marking is at once representative of the Underground system, the bus network, the colours of the Union flag and London itself. In recent years, the 'Cool Britannia' slogan and variations on the austerity-chic motto 'Keep Calm and Carry On' have created a revival of patriotic imagery applied to every conceivable object. In 2012 the souvenir trade marketed its London products harder than ever, for both the Queen's Diamond Jubilee and the London Olympic and Paralympic Games.

'An exclusive London Transport gift says "London" to the whole world.'[1]

London Underground motifs are an established feature of the merchandise available to tourists seeking souvenirs of London. Such is the significance of the logo that it may influence the branding of the retail outlet as well (LEFT).

By the 1970s, the London Transport roundel was established as a brand in the retailing of souvenirs.

If we return to one of the themes in the introduction, that of heraldry and the use of symbols to organize groups, it is a short step to see how the devices and images of national identity and capital city are eminently saleable in this time of intense consumerism. The blue-and-red bulls-eye/roundel has featured in London memorabilia for some decades, and is now prominent as a brand. Souvenir goods to be marked with the roundel are carefully vetted and strictly licensed; imitations appear from time to time. This chapter features the official merchandise which carries the bar and circle to all parts of the world.

London Transport became aware of the potential for retailing its brand in the 1920s, when it began to sell reproduction posters following requests from admiring travellers. It opened a showroom/shop in its headquarters building at 55 Broadway, Westminster, above St James's Park station. Publicity Officer Harold Hutchison, whose job it was to commission new posters from 1949 to 1966, was also a writer who compiled several guides to London for travellers. These, too, were sold by the organization for the benefit of travellers. In the 1960s, histories of the Underground began to be published in association with London Transport, and so the retail activities progressed. A shop maintained by the London Transport Publicity Office near Edgware Road, Marylebone, offered a stock of posters, postcards and books as part of its wider public-relations programme. Promotion of the bar and circle as a tourist brand and commercial venture really took off in the 1970s, when historic London Transport objects removed from the defunct Museum of British Transport were temporarily relocated to Syon Park, West London, to the nascent London Transport Museum.[2]

The connections between London Transport, city and tourist would be exploited in many ways in order to obtain the best value from the organization's heritage. At first the range of goods was comparable to that in any visitor-attraction shop, tending towards frank and direct uses of the Underground bulls-eye on generic giftware – ashtrays, wall plaques, key chains, tea towels, clothing – or on imitations of real objects such as badges and station nameboards.[3] Gift shops were based at St James's Park station, and at Charing Cross from 1979. From 1980, the London Transport Museum took control of the parent organization's residual retail activities.

For many years John Lovelock and Vera Thompson directed Garnier Signs, a company with French origins founded in east London in 1885 to make nameplates for shopfronts. Later settled in a group of factory buildings in Willesden, north-west London, Garnier manufactured station nameboards for London Transport. Shortages of steel, and the increasing demand for souvenirs, led to the idea of reproducing the signs in miniature for sale to tourists and transport enthusiasts. Most central London Underground stations were featured in the hugely successful range, made from the scale of a fridge magnet and key fob to a convincingly large plate. One particularly intrepid London Underground employee placed orders with Garnier for exclusive products to be sold at enthusiasts' fairs, and he also traded in real transport signs which had been rejected by the customer. Besides vitreous-enamel giftware, Garnier experimented with other objects that could carry the bar-and-circle symbol. Their range grew to encompass vinyl stickers, mirrors, ceramic mugs, thimbles, bells and plates – all decorated with the London Transport bulls-eye and a station name or directional text which would appeal to souvenir hunters. A trip to Garnier began with a hot cup of tea and proceeded through their huddled sheds from the damp, colourful screen printing and spraying rooms to the heat of the kilns, which fused the enamel 'frit' onto the steel plates at something over 1400°F (800°C). Among its thousands of other products were miniature street and railway signs, reproduction advertising plaques, tinplate postcards, 'pop' and Union-flag motifs. The company was absorbed by another manufacturer in 1998, and large-scale production of the miniature signs ceased.

Driven by comprehensive retailing strategies, promotion of the logo as a product in itself and in order to brand merchandise has become increasingly smart. Through licensing programmes and in-house development, there are gifts and toys for children marked *Underground* in the lower-level price brackets; a range of toy train sets was sold under the bar-and-circle logo *Underground Ernie*. There are games and crockery and chocolate bars and underwear for adults, sporting symbols with the word 'Angel'. 'Mind the Gap', a message which for many years was broadcast automatically at several central London stations, has become a slogan in its own right, adorning roundels throughout the product ranges.

The main retail outlet for roundel-themed goods is the London Transport Museum, which has mined its own collections for iconic images to reproduce. It has considered how important historical artefacts can be transformed or re-contextualized into attractive objects for the higher levels of merchandise. In a very postmodern way, images designed for beauty and efficiency in the context of travel have moved into another sphere of creativity, where they have been abstracted, replicated, multiplied and applied to contemporary designs. Textile moquettes for covering tube-car seats carry the bulls-eye into furniture design. The

Tourists and enthusiasts alike really could own a piece of London Underground when they bought merchandise produced in the same factory as the official tube station signs.

A massive variety of objects have, at some time, been branded with the roundel as part of official retail initiatives.

homewares design and sourcing company BlissHome has worked with Transport for London to produce goods based on the designs of the inter-war period. Besides these innovations, postcards and posters continue to feature bulls-eye and roundel artworks. At the London Design Festival in September 2011, samples of replica roundel signs were displayed at various venues, including the Victoria and Albert Museum. The replica signs were launched to the design and collector markets, allowing people to actually buy original 'enamel' signs.[4] Presently, a mug or T-shirt, coaster or mouse mat, is available to be branded with any London Underground/ Overground station or tram stop name, in the appropriate modal colour. For a somewhat greater expenditure, it is possible to buy an authentic London Underground vitreous-enamel roundel, labelled with a station or stop name.[5] For London Underground's 150th birthday in 2013, new product ranges are being created according to precise brand guidelines.

The visual culture of London Transport has inspired many designers in their own work. It has also been subject to imitators and counterfeiters selling non-approved products. Transport for London continues to protect its trademarks and brands vigorously. Nevertheless, the fear of Misha Black (erstwhile design consultant to the Underground) that the bar and circle be used in applications as inappropriate as cheap souvenir underwear remains a possibility today, as we will see in Chapter 11.

One of the four 'Blueprint' London Underground 150th anniversary plates produced in hand-gilded bone china by designer ceramics company The New English, based in Stoke on Trent.

Pieces from the BlissHome 'Underground' homewares range for Transport for London.

10

ADMIRERS AND IMITATORS

Over the last century, the strong brand and visual identity of London Transport has had a major impact on other transport operators, organizations and businesses, both at home and abroad. Earlier in this book, it was evident that, despite its startling originality, the symbol had sources in other places – for example, Samuel Plimsoll's load line for ships and the YMCA/YWCA triangle and bar. In the ebb and flow of design and business, war and peace, so the bar and circle has had parallels with other, similar, devices and been admired and adapted for many different purposes. This chapter looks at the many symbols and brands that display the clear influence of the London Transport bar and circle.

TRANSPORT AT HOME

For the originators of the Underground Group and London Transport, it made good publicity sense to share their business practice with other transport providers. Where they did not actively do this, the bar and circle was nevertheless established as shorthand for 'transport' by the 1920s, throughout Britain and the empire. We have already seen in the Metropolitan Railway an early example of an operator who adapted the device for its own symbol (see p. 30). Elsewhere, its influence can be seen in Southern Railway's 'target' station nameboard, clearly derived from the bulls-eye,[1] and in a nameboard used by the London, Midland and Scottish Railway, known as the 'hawkseye', which used the outline of the bulls-eye. In Glasgow, the city's subway directly adopted the bulls-eye, the system being renamed 'Underground' in 1936; half-bulls-eyes form some station exteriors. Several motor-bus and coach operators in other British towns and cities, from Cornwall to Yorkshire, also took the bar-and-circle form for their insignia.

Southern Railway (England) 'target' nameboard (TOP), and London, Midland and Scottish Railway 'hawkseye' nameboard (ABOVE), both 1930s.

Odd spin-offs from the companies that London Transport had absorbed in the 1930s through its predecessors included Northmet (the North Metropolitan Electric Power Supply Company), which generated traction current for trams and supplied electricity to parts of the northern Home Counties. Northmet also had showrooms for the sale of electrical appliances in Wood Green. After nationalization of the generating industry, the logo continued in use for some years by Eastern Electricity. London Transport attempted to block this use.

In recent times, careful control of how the roundel is used has limited the possibilities for imitation, meaning that seemingly similar devices have different roots. For instance, the current trading mark of Southern Railway Ltd (2004–) is derived from the logotype and signs of the former Southern Railway (1923–47).

The Northmet logo, *c.* 1938.

Official stamp of the Glasgow Corporation Transport Underground system, and a station exterior with half-bar and circle, both 1960s.

PARIS *et sa* BANLIEUE
par les AUTOBUS
et le MÉTRO

R.A.T.P

Para viajar por Madrid

TOMAD
el

METRO

Comprad

TACOS de
10 BILLETES

en cualquier taquilla del Metro

Symbols inspired by the London Transport
logo have frequently been adopted by other
transport operators. CLOCKWISE FROM TOP
LEFT: Paris, France; Hyderabad, India;
Barcelona, Spain; Tokyo, Japan; Madrid, Spain.

So far this story has been confined to London and Britain. However, the capital's chief transport operator has never regarded itself in these limited terms. When London was the centre of an empire, and when its citizens travelled for peaceful reasons, the phenomenon of its transport system spread far and wide. As we have seen, in times of war the bar and circle accompanied troops as a totem of homeland and belonging.

Ever the entrepreneur, London Transport's first Chairman, Lord Ashfield, saw the publicity value in sharing the bar and circle with contacts overseas. When he was not personally forging links with other transport operators – he had many business colleagues in North America and elsewhere, and was Chairman of the Havana Railways of Cuba – observers of his system noted the great efficiency of the symbol in communicating a message of transportation service. Lord Ashfield responded to requests for Underground posters to be sent to other operators as examples of good publicity.[2] London Transport was a consultant on an international scale, taking the bar and circle to, for example, Gibraltar, Iran, Russia and Canada. Ashfield and his deputy Frank Pick were given honorary awards by Josef Stalin in recognition of their advice on the construction of the Moscow Metro. Buses were sent on official tours to several countries; recruitment teams visited distant islands to secure employees at a time of staff shortages during the 1950s.

The first recorded example of the bar and circle travelling overseas was with the large-scale shipment of London General Omnibus Company (LGOC) vehicles to France during the First World War. After the conflict in 1918, LGOC buses were sold to Athens, Greece. To manufacture road vehicles the Underground Group had formed the Associated Equipment Company (AEC). AEC was later sold to another vehicle producer; however, it continued using the bar-and-circle symbols that were its trademarks for many years, in domestic and export contexts. London Transport and the main-line railway companies were models for systems in former colonies on the continents of Africa, Australia and Asia; bar-and-circle station nameboards of various forms are still to be found on several systems. Other networks such as Nyasaland Transport[3] or the buses of [His Exalted Highness] The Nizam's [Guaranteed] State Railway in Hyderabad, India,[4] are now changed and have ceased to use the symbol. The Second World War brought the bulls-eye to the Far East, alongside troop movements. Subway companies in Madrid and Barcelona, Spain, adapted the London Metropolitan Railway's diamond-and-bar sign (see p. 30), while the Paris

Several railway systems around the world have created versions of the bar and circle to identify their services. TOP TO BOTTOM: Chicago, USA; Wellington, New Zealand; Poland Railways; Cuba.

Metropolitain used several symbols with a resemblance to the bar and circle. Since 1945, developing subway systems in many countries have chosen a variation on the form of circle and rectangle to identify their services; a selection is shown here. Abstracted typographically, the round or ovoid form suggests the city and the horizontal elements are the routes across it.

COMMERCE

Away from transportation, the simplicity of a bar and circle and the red and blue colours have been attractive to commerce, and many brands have echoed the London Transport symbol, deliberately or otherwise. Cars were produced in Japan under the Datsun brand name from 1932–3; the company later changed its worldwide car marque to Nissan. Its device is based on the Japanese flag, with its red solar disc. Martini vermouth, created by Martini & Rossi in Turin, Italy, registered their 'bar and ball' trademark in 1929, reproducing it in a variety of colours according to product. The red, white and blue variety of the Martini logo is now also associated with sponsorship of motor racing. The British Robbialac Paint Company established a brand in India which used a direct copy of the red-and-blue bulls-eye. In west London, Job's Dairy suppliers used the symbol in the 1930s, while a bar-and-circle motif marked publicity issued by the Workers' Educational Association (WEA). There are still trademarks in Greece which directly resemble the red-and-blue Underground logo; one for FAGE (founded 1926) can be seen on Total dairy products in food shops around the world.

In the next, and final, chapter, we review how the significance of the bar and circle has echoed through culture and counter-culture over the decades, identifying London as an international capital city – a place of significant cultural diversity and cultural production, modernity and fashion – in fields including music, film, fashion and political activities.

Tube Suit by David Samuel (2009).

11

GOING UNDERGROUND

We have seen how brand became increasingly important in the marketing of London's transport provision in the late twentieth century. London Transport's symbol has endured because it works exceptionally well as a tool of organization and identification. The power of brands – commercially, industrially, politically and culturally – inevitably has its inverse: the potential for subversion. This is not new; recognizable symbols of authority and establishment have always been appropriated to convey alternative messages and viewpoints. What is different is the omnipresence of brands in electronic media, meaning they are now much more easily recognizable to audiences on a global scale and readily accessible for manipulation. The bar-and-circle symbol is an eminent candidate for such uses.

For Frank Pick, the Underground – that is to say, the group of railway, bus, tram and trolleybus networks and associated infrastructure in London – was an antidote to the dirt and confusion of real life as he perceived it. The Underground was a Utopia in the making, created from the best design and art, architecture, engineering and administration: total, complete. Pick used the presence of a coherent transport network in London as a medium by which the city could be ordered, and its citizens transported – literally, intellectually, metaphorically, spiritually – all under the sign of the bar and circle. But there is another important story, the inverse of Pick's dream, which weaves its way through the real city and imagined worlds, through society and art, lifestyle and politics.

To understand this extraordinary spectrum of cultural expressions we must first look to nineteenth-century literature, which suggests a very different set of associations to implicate the bar and circle. In 1864 the Russian novelist Fyodor Dostoyevsky published *Notes from Underground*, in which he uses 'underground' as a conceptual alternative to bright city spaces peopled with noisy travellers and colourful images. This was the narrative of an isolated man who had retreated to a tiny corner of existence, dark and angry, out of step with imperial Russian society. H.G. Wells, who for some years lived in an apartment block above Baker Street Underground station, was skilled at creating other worlds which were both critical of his own time and prophetic of things to come. *The Time Machine* (1895) divides society into a vulnerable elite who live on the surface and indulge in a leisurely, aesthetically perfect existence, and another, predatory group who have a servile life below the earth's surface. Again, this is a repositioning of the world called 'underground' to something other – out of place, only partly known. Resistance groups during wartime have been referred to as 'the underground'. When the music and fashion worlds of the mid-1960s reacted against the establishment they deemed themselves 'underground' and gave their various expressions suitably subterranean names – the band The Velvet Underground is an obvious example. Film making has a long history of underground activities and working outside of the mainstream industry, while underground comics and magazines are a method of communicating opinions and narratives which for one reason or another are excluded from the general press. Postmodernity transforms political and cultural polarities in complex ways, inverting and distorting, confusing and rehabilitating: anything goes. Dark becomes light, serious becomes ironic, deep content slides into shallow surface. This chapter illustrates a host of adaptations, appropriations and reinterpretations of the bar and circle as various forms of culture evolve and restate themselves.

POP

When Britain celebrated other cultures that it had encountered during the Second World War, and took a critical look at its own society in the 1960s, London came alive with appropriations of designs associated with patriotism – chiefly, the Union flag – and iconography related to the military or Victoriana. These symbols were taken up in popular culture by music groups and their followers. One dominant mark was the Royal Air Force roundel, which came to be associated with the mod[ernist] movement's music and the tribal clothes – sweatshirts, parkas – of its participants. With revivals of the style, mod icons have been merged with references to the The Jam's song *Going Underground* and bulls-eye badges circulated showing this and other music-group names. Somewhere along the way, the heady mix of underground, London and the red, white and blue of the pop-art target (recalling the work of artists Peter Blake and Jasper Johns)

The 1960s mod movement appropriated the Royal Air Force roundel, an arrangement of concentric circles in blue, white and red.

spawned symbols intended to inspire associations with 'swinging' London. The record sleeve of the hit song *Finchley Central* by The New Vaudeville Band (1967) showed the station nameboard. Other music-group names feature on bulls-eye badges produced for their fans. American flautist Herbie Mann issued a long-playing album called *London Underground* (1974), while Gary Numan's band Tubeway Army was marketed with a red roundel in 1979. Links with music continue: S-Express offered a visual essay on the bulls-eye, which was in keeping with their creative sampling of music genres (1988); American DJ Armand van Helden issued music under the pseudonym The Mole People – a reference to Jennifer Toth's 1995 book *The Mole People: Life in the Tunnels Beneath New York City*, which itself recalls the science fiction of H.G. Wells in *The Time Machine*, and the 1956 film *The Mole People*. The urban nature of the bar and circle makes it attractive to record labels and retailers. One recent innovation has seen Transport for London license a trademark for Waterloo Records in Austin, Texas, and lease it back to the company. In films and television productions the bulls-eye is used to lend authenticity, offering a clear and immediate location and historical setting, and associating the plot with London, England or Britishness, whether the subject is creatures from outer space or international espionage.

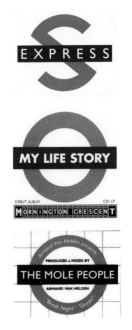

ABOVE: Appropriations of the bar and circle in pop-music cover artwork and merchandise.

LEFT: Transport for London licensed the trademark for use by Waterloo Records in Austin, Texas.

FASHION, NIGHTLIFE AND ART

Fashion stores and clothing labels around the world identify their brands with the bar and circle to impart a 'cool'/London style to their wares, or to suggest that by being 'underground' they are fashion leaders. History has shown the eye-catching value of red, white and blue in uniforms, and it is no less effective on casual T-shirts. Music and fashion come together in pubs, bars and clubs. The idea of these dark, night-time places being haunts for alternative cultures is by no means new; however, it is only in the late twentieth century that such establishments began to adopt the bulls-eye as a totem of their activities, in order to appear fashionable or 'underground'. Related symbols appear, too, in art. Two examples from outside the Art on the Underground programme are the *Tube Suit* by artist David Samuel (2009; see p. 154), and designer and artist Anna Garforth's living tube sign (2011).

The symbol used in nightlife (ABOVE), and to publicize fashion brands (RIGHT).

SOCIAL AND POLITICAL GROUPS

Associations with London and the London Transport symbol find their way into the activities of various kinds of organized groups. In this way such collectives relate themselves directly to the city, or to particular places and events in the city which have historical or cultural meaning.

A station nameboard has been adopted as the motif of the Stairway to Heaven Memorial Trust, a project to create a permanent tribute for the Bethnal Green Tube Disaster of 1943 in which 173 died in a crush to enter the station as an air-raid shelter. The London Passenger Transport League flourished in the years 1983–8, and identified themselves by a symbol that can be compared to the bar and circle or a Celtic sun-wheel cross, which uses the form of four initials as the London Passenger Transport Board (LPTB) had done.[1] In the sport of skateboarding, the bar and circle in its counter-cultural 'underground' context has been associated with manufacturers and retailers of boards.

The global Occupy movement camp at St Paul's Churchyard, near the London Stock Exchange, used the red-and-blue bar and circle to announce its activities until late 2011, when Transport for London asked for this use to cease.[2] There are other historical links between political themes and the London Transport symbol.

The bar and circle has appeared in diverse uses from social and political groups to sports brands. ABOVE, FROM TOP: The former London Passenger Transport League research and publishing mark; Hope not Hate, campaigners against racism and fascism; a North American skateboard brand. LEFT: The offices of the Occupied Times newspaper at St Paul's Churchyard camp in London, 2011.

OPPOSITE: Appropriations of the bar and circle found around the world.

Individuals and businesses around the world may see the bar and circle simply as a recognizable and efficient symbol with which to convey a particular message: a selection of examples is illustrated opposite. Whatever the value of these implied associations, there is the potential to undermine the reputation of Transport for London. How should such uses be controlled? The companies that own the intellectual property rights to brands would certainly argue that these rights afford them protection from plagiarism and misrepresentation; they state that they will pursue any infringement of their brand rights because it has the potential to damage their reputations. Transport for London makes every effort to protect its marks both in the UK and in many countries around the world. The organization is very careful to ensure that its trademarks and brands are licensed only for approved uses: this book, for instance, was licensed before it could be published. The converse argument is that by advancing their trademarks in the competitive arena of selling products to consumers, businesses are exposing themselves to comment and the language of symbols can be used against them to convey equally succinct messages of anti-corporatism and anti-capitalism. We cannot resolve these questions here, but we can marvel at the ingenuity of these uses.

CONCLUSION

As centres of culture, hosts for world's fairs and expositions or International Olympic Games, cities now brand themselves with a logo. An iconic cultural building or typographical symbol will recur in the diffusion of media advancing one location or another to prospective leisure and business visitors. Entire countries adopt a universally readable symbol to surmount language barriers. Metro and subway systems around the world have related forms of logotype, so as to be recognized by both tourists and residents. Brands migrate easily – some London bus services are presently operated and branded by French transport organization Groupe RATP, and by Dutch Railways (Nederlandse Spoorwegen). Beyond London, national groups acquire the infrastructure of other nations in periods of economic change, and their brands follow. Museums, universities, charities and food retailers choose trading marks as important elements of their enterprise strategies, 'refreshing' these marks at intervals to retain the public's interest.

Originally intended to identify the transport network of a private organization, the bar-and-circle symbol has, over a century, become part of, and a shorthand for, the personality of London, as a city and world centre of social, political and cultural activity. In a two-colour, easy-to-spot form, the bar and circle is seen as a symbol for *our* London. When we think of the capital from some other place, it is there to represent the metropolis to us as much as the red telephone kiosk, Tower Bridge, a guardsman, beefeater or post-office pillar box. Through its association with tourism and the patriotic colours of its Underground form, the bar and circle also communicates 'Britain' to travellers (although, of course, there is very much more to the British Isles than London itself).

The Underground Group was highly innovative in advancing a symbol for its services in a period when advertising and printed media still relied very much on text to communicate its message. Frank Pick retained overall supervision of publicity matters throughout his career with the Underground and London Transport. The organization was controlled by a relatively small number of people at this early stage in its development. It is certain that Pick's superior, Lord Ashfield, was instrumental in directing a team of staff towards activities which resulted in the emergence of the symbol, but its early development was more an organic evolutionary process – part trial and error – than a planned programme of change. The device emerged from the work of a well-travelled, bright, talented and hardworking management team backed by American and European financiers. It benefited from the economic and aesthetic endeavours of Frank Pick – directed by his superior, Lord Ashfield – and also from Pick's prescience in inviting calligrapher Edward Johnston to refine and develop the design for use throughout a rapidly expanding business. Johnston, Pick, Ashfield and their team created one of the first universal brand marks. With the carefully considered proportions originated by Johnston, the bar and circle was gifted with a harmony of horizontal and vertical dynamics. Where other complex brand marks have failed, the bar-and-circle symbol has lasted because it is very simple, an archetype. The spare simplicity of Johnston's logo unites exemplary practice from millennia of hand-crafted letter making with an emerging sympathy for machine-made pure lines and shapes that was characteristic of the modernist period in design, and which has remained current for over a century. Within a few years, Johnston's design was sufficiently well established in the visual environment of London that it was possible to communicate its presence and meaning without words. Under the influence of experimental artists and designers, including Man Ray and Hans Schleger, the symbol was transformed into a universal graphical metonym for London's transport. Awareness of the symbol's value grew over time. Through unification, nationalization and now privatization, design activity has been continued as a means of maintaining order in an expanding and changing business. It is this enduring search for identity that sets the work forth as an example to successive generations of passengers, operators and designers.

We have now delved into the history of the bar and circle in considerable detail, but what of the future? Transport for London publishes its *Corporate Design Standards* 'for use by staff, suppliers and design agencies involved in graphic design and layout'.[1] By referring to these documents, every detail of the correct colour and typographical use of each modal roundel can be obtained. A study of the guidelines reveals that each symbol must be shown with what is termed an 'exclusion zone'. This is the area of flat colour on which the roundel is placed, and it is so arranged to prevent other typography from reducing the visual legibility of the design. There are two formats for this exclusion zone. The first is near-square, featuring the roundel only; the second provides for a logotype alongside the roundel. This latter form has proved very useful in recent years, with the advent of corporate sponsorship. In the two examples to date – Barclays Cycle Hire and Emirates Air Line – the logotype adjacent to the roundel has actually encompassed it to form a new symbol. This practice brings potential for the symbol to be a clearly defined component of a more complex family of brands. Given the perception that the bar and circle is part of all our 'Londons', there is strong feeling about encroachment on the exclusivity of the symbol.

Whatever our view on the association of the roundel with corporate sponsors, we have to realize that it was itself the product of a commercial venture, and so it is appropriate that it continues to be used in this way. Linking it with other businesses firmly establishes it as a brand in the generally understood commercial sense. This is happening to many organizations who had previously thought themselves above, or outside, the marketplace: police forces, the armed services and local authorities, for instance. Corporate sponsorship demonstrates the resilience and continuing commercial and graphic relevance of the bar-and-circle symbol. Applications for mobile devices offer infinite possibilities for accessing incredible volumes of data feeds to advise users of bus running times, the nearest taxis or available cycles for hire. For these 'apps' to easily show their purpose, the roundel – and other Transport for London 'properties' – is a desirable feature. How its protected status can be maintained in the world of downloadable media remains to be fully appreciated, but one way to meet the desire for a connection with the roundel is the innovation of personalized goods featuring the symbol, from the London Transport Museum and Transport for London shop websites.[2]

Some brands are always associated with a particular colour. Consider the long heritage of the Coca-Cola Company of Atlanta, USA, and red is prominent in the packaging and advertising.[3] For most of its existence, the Shell group of energy and petrochemicals companies has identified itself with a red-and-yellow symbol, while international oil and gas company BP uses green and yellow. Other organizations, such as Nissan, have shifted from colour to metallic effects for their trading devices. Wolff Olins's logos for the London 2012 Olympic Games and Paralympic Games were based on the concept of a logo that was also a template, into which many different graphic and photographic images could be inserted for special events, and by sponsors.[4] The bar and circle seems to work in any colour or context – even as an embossed, colourless symbol. Transport for

London has coloured modal roundels on file for use in new projects. Published transport strategies for London take into consideration the capital's needs up to the year 2031. When Conran Design Group speculated about possible future uses in their 2017 portfolio of images, hidden away among their fantasy roundels was one which may be in use to identify common service standards if the Mayor's plans for enhancement of the London suburban rail network are approved.[5] Future London rail projects circulated in the media include BAA Ltd's Airtrack; Wandsworth Council's Airtrack-Lite; and the further extension of the Thameslink network, Bakerloo line and the 'Chelsea–Hackney line'. What roundels might these ventures obtain, should they proceed? As the capital inevitably sees more infrastructural development, the bar and circle will infiltrate every part of the capital – truly a logo for London.

NOTES

INTRODUCTION

1. F. Pick, *Design in Transport*. A lecture given to the Design & Industries Association Birmingham branch, 8 December 1933. Transport for London Corporate Archives (TfLCA) ref. LT 535/28/1.
2. H.F. Hutchison (Publicity Officer, London Transport Executive), 'Underground and London Transport' [internal report], 31 January 1949. TfLCA ref. LT 371/073, p. 2.
3. This anecdote was given by Pat Schleger, wife of Hans Schleger, in conversation with the author, 26 April 1995. Samuel Plimsoll (1824–98) created the load line which takes his name to show the level to which a ship could be loaded without affecting its stability. A historian of Plimsoll claimed that the mark was adapted from a symbol used on Sardinian fishing vessels of the twelfth and thirteenth centuries; see D. Masters, *The Plimsoll Mark*. London: Cassell & Co., 1955, p. 6.
4. Professor Sir Ernst Gombrich (1909–2001) in a letter to the author, 7 March 1996, stated: 'I have always assumed that [the logo] represents the ultimate abbreviation or simplification of its intended significance: the circle shows the area of London that is crossed by the Underground railway. You may notice that even the standard map of the network represents a simplification; the logo takes it one step further.'
5. On the first map of *UndergrounD*-branded railways, published at the time of the Franco–British Exhibition in 1908, the colours of the lines were as follows: Bakerloo – brown, Central London – light blue, City & South London – black, District – green, Great Northern & City – orange, Hampstead – dark blue, Metropolitan – red, Piccadilly – yellow.
6. TfLCA ref. LT 606/26.

CHAPTER 1

1. A drawing of the proposed design was submitted to the LGOC board on 30 March 1905: 'Mr Crane being in attendance submitted a coloured design for a trademark which was approved and Mr Crane was instructed to register the same.' London Metropolitan Archives (LMA) ref. ACC/1297/ LGOC/01/031 Board Meetings File 1905–1906, minute number 60398. The design was revised shortly afterwards (27 April 1905) so that it could be registered as a trademark.
2. The Underground Electric Railways of London Ltd was created on 9 April 1902.
3. *The Builder*, 17 March 1906, p. 28. The decorations comprised various arrangements of blue, mauve, green, brown and amber tiles. The best resource for studying these tile patterns is D. Rose, *Tiles of the Unexpected*. Harrow Weald: Capital Transport Publishing, 2007.
4. London Transport Publicity Office, *Origins of the London Transport Bulls-eye*, 11 May 1955, p. 2.
5. This is Justin Howes's citation of Edward Johnston's lecture on 'Signwriting' of 28 September 1906, originally quoted in H. Child and J. Howes (eds), *Edward Johnston: Lessons in Formal Writing*. London: Lund Humphries, 1986, p. 94.
6. The Baker Street & Waterloo Railway opened on 10 March 1906; the Great Northern, Piccadilly & Brompton Railway on 15 December 1906; and the Charing Cross, Euston & Hampstead Railway on 22 June 1907.
7. The first meeting of the London Passenger Traffic Conference took place on 22 July 1907.
8. Harry Ford was consultant architect to the District Railway subsidiary of the Underground Group, 1899–1911. He wrote to the *Daily Express* in 1938 to express his dismay at the newspaper reporting the award of a CBE to Edward Johnston with an attribution of the *UndergrounD* logotype to Johnston. The image reproduced was in fact the Johnston redraft of the original 1908 design by Ford.
9. The events were recalled by William H. Hilton in 1955. Hilton had joined the District Railway in 1905. As a junior clerk he worked with Joseph Carter, and would have been close to the procurement of station signs and other items from uniforms to tickets. In 1908, Hilton was appointed one of two staff in the newly formed buying section of the District Railway, and in August 1955 he retired as Purchasing Officer for London Transport.
10. The Paris Metro nameboards had letters 8 inches (20 cm) tall, and were shown on clear space 8–12 feet (2.44–3.66 m) high by 6 feet (1.83 m) wide, at frequent intervals along platforms.
11. H.T. (Harry) Carr, Assistant Publicity Officer to Christian Barman 1935–41, Acting Publicity Officer 1941–6.
12. C. Barman, *The Man Who Built London Transport: A Biography of Frank Pick*. Newton Abbot: David & Charles, 1979, pp. 29–30.
13. Joseph Carter was rewarded for his special services on estate work early in 1908. LMA ref. MDR/01/010 minute 6737, 26 February 1908.
14. 'Posters are Our Silent Passengers: 490,000–', *Pennyfare* [War Series], no. 79, April 1946, p. 751.
15. Noted in a letter from Walter Gott to Sir John Elliot, Chairman – London Transport Executive, 20 December 1954.
16. 'Mr H.T. Carr Retires: In Publicity 38 Years', *Pennyfare* [War Series], no. 89, February 1947, p. 913.

17. Underground Group board minute 520 of 29 July 1908 notes an approval for expenditure on 'enamelled nameplates for all the stations of the joint railways'. LMA ref. ACC1297 etc CXEH 1/2. A further minute, 687 of 12 August 1908, records the request 'to expend the sum of £5000 [about £407,000 in 2010] in providing fire proof hoardings on the walls of the tunnel stations (and other stations where necessary) in order to improve the display of advertisements and *station name plates*'. LMA ref. ACC/1297/MDR/01/010 Board and General Meetings File 1907–1911. By 1909, a visitor to the District Railway could report that the 'name of each station [is] now shown in white letters upon a blue panel resting on a large red target with a white background … repeated several times on each platform'; see G.W.J. Potter, 'The District Railway of to-day', *The Railway Magazine*, vol. 24, May 1909, p. 386.

18. A handbill of 1912 promoting the London General Omnibus Company bus route 84 is almost certainly the first printed item to carry an Underground Group-designed ring-and-bar symbol.

19. C. Barman, 'How to make a typographical impact with facias and trade marks'. *Advertiser's Weekly*, 12 May 1955, pp. 334, 336, 338.

20. The Deutscher Werkbund was an association of artists, designers and architects formed in Munich, Germany, in 1907. For the history of the Design & Industries Association, see www.dia.org.uk/page/AboutUs/Nothing_Need_be_Ugly

21. Frank Pick, in a talk to students of the Leicester School of Art, cited in Barman 1955, *op. cit.* (n.19), p. 336. The lettering had been commissioned from Eric Gill in 1903.

22. A manuscript of the typeface, annotated 'first drawing', is dated 6 February 1916. Crafts Study Centre, University for the Creative Arts, Farnham: Edward Johnston Collection & Archive (CSC) ref. C.86.125.

23. P. Johnston, *Edward Johnston*. London: Faber and Faber, 1959, p. 205.

24. In the words of Marshall McLuhan, 'The goose quill put an end to talk. It abolished mystery; it gave architecture and towns; it brought roads and armies, bureaucracy. It was the basic metaphor with which the cycle of civilisation began, the step from the dark into the light of the mind. The hand that filled the parchment page built a city.' M. McLuhan and Q. Fiore with J. Agel, *The Medium is the Massage*. Harmondsworth: Penguin, 1967, p. 48.

25. Johnston, *op. cit.* (n.23), p. 201. The italics are reproduced from the original text.

26. *Ibid.*

27. The Underground bar and circle was registered at the Patent Office as a design for publicity and station-nameboard use on 17 March 1917; patent numbers 659814–25. National Archives ref. BT/53/35.

CHAPTER 2

1. See K. Garland, *Mr Beck's Underground Map*. Harrow Weald: Capital Transport Publishing, 1994.

2. H.F. Hutchison, '*Art For All*'. *An exhibition of posters & their originals produced by London Transport 1908–1949*. London: Arts Council of Great Britain, 1949, p. 22.

3. *Ibid.*, p. 24.

4. It was Meynell who acted for Pick in persuading his friend Edward Johnston to design a typeface for the Underground Group, and Meynell also who continued to bring work to Johnston for many years. See Johnston, *op. cit.* (ch.1, n.23), esp. pp. 190–95 and 198–9.

5. London General Country Services began operation in May 1933.

6. H.T. Carr to Edward Johnston, 20 March 1931, CSC ref. 2/133. The General Busways and Green Line Coachways titles were used in London Passenger Transport Board publicity in late 1933.

7. Edward Johnston to H.T. Carr, 21 April 1931, CSC ref. 2/135.

8. Carr to Johnston, 22 April 1931, CSC ref. 2/136.

9. Carr to Johnston, 30 April 1931. CSC ref. 2/137.

10. Carr to Johnston, 19 April 1932. CSC ref. 2/141.

11. Johnston to Carr, 20 April 1932. CSC ref. 2/143.

12. Carr to Johnston, 22 June 1932. CSC ref. 2/144.

13. The date of the commission was 3 April 1933. At this time, Edward Johnston was in correspondence with G.W. Duncan at the Underground. Report delivered 14 May 1933, CSC ref. 2/147.

14. Johnston to Carr, 14 May 1933, p. 3, CSC ref. 2/147.

15. *Ibid.*, p. 4.

16. Carr to Johnston, 5 October 1933, CSC ref. 2/148.

17. Johnston to Carr, 5 October 1933, CSC ref. 2/149.

18. Johnston to Carr, 8 October 1933, CSC ref. 2/149.

19. Edward Johnston to H.T. Carr, 'Report (continued) on the Five "bulls-eye" (UndergrounD, Green LinE, GeneraL, TrolleybuS, TramwayS) and on the London Transport Bulls-eye Design, followed by a Report on the plain "Labels" (which have the words "London Transport" appended)'. 30 October 1933, private paper.

20. Edward Johnston to H.T. Carr, 'Report on the bulls-eye designs … as surcharged with the words "LONDON TRANSPORT"'. 29 October 1933, private paper.

21. *Ibid.*

22. Hutchison, *op. cit.* (intr., n.2), p. 3.

23. Johnston to Carr, 3 December 1933, CSC ref. 2/160.

24. The fount produced by Percy J. Delf Smith for the Underground was, like Edward Johnston's Railway Block Letter, hand drawn and based on classical prototypes. Delf Smith reintroduced what Johnston had removed – the serifs, or small extensions, on the ends of the letters. The letters were upper case only. Signs using Delf Smith's fount seem to have been limited to a few Underground stations, including Sudbury Town, Manor House, Oakwood, Cockfosters and Boston Manor. He also designed lettering for the Heal & Son furniture company.

25. London Transport experimented with fixed stops on bus route number 27, Euston Road to Seven Sisters Corner, Tottenham, from 20 March 1935.

26. Recalled by Pat Schleger in conversation with the author, 26 April 1995.

27. *Ibid.*

28. A pair of tram lines ran under London's Kingsway, connecting north London routes with those south of the river. Two 'stations' were provided at Holborn and Aldwych for travellers to join the trams. Large bar-and-circle station nameboards were provided, like the railway examples but with blue rings and black bars.

29. These route maps at the foot of the escalators or top of the stairs are officially called bifurcation diagrams because they indicate the separate directions to be taken by travellers in opposite directions.

30. H.T. Carr and W.P.N. Edwards, 'Report on the standardisation of signs, notices and maps – Railways'. London Passenger Transport Board, 8 August 1938.

CHAPTER 3

1. These were the 41st, 42nd, 43rd, 44th, 45th, 46th and 60th battalions, formed in 1940 and stood down in 1946.

2. 'Our Sign Enters Italy'. *Pennyfare* [War Series], no. 53, February 1944, p. 417, and 'Bulls-eye May Enter Berlin as Gunners' Emblem'. *Pennyfare* [War Series], no. 61, October 1944, p. 481.

3. 'Symbol of Their Hopes'. *Pennyfare* [War Series], no. 55, April 1944, p. 440.

CHAPTER 4

1. Bryce Beaumont, former London Transport Publicity Officer, to the author, 24 October 1988.

2. New Towns served by London Transport were Stevenage, Hertfordshire (designated as a New Town, 1946); Crawley, West Sussex (1947); Hemel Hempstead, Hertfordshire (1947); Harlow, Essex (1947); Hatfield, Hertfordshire (1948); and Welwyn Garden City, Hertfordshire (1947).

3. Publicity Officer Harold Hutchison said to A.B.B. (later Sir Alec) Valentine, then a member of the London Transport Executive, that they should not get involved in advising the Railway Executive on use of signs. Even so, a subsequent meeting with V.M. Barrington-Ward, who supervised railway operation for the Railway Executive, saw 'sample drawings of the new symbol of British Railways' reviewed. The colours of the new symbol were listed as follows: Southern Region – white lettering on green; Western Region – cream lettering on chocolate; Eastern Region – white lettering on blue; North-Eastern Region – black lettering on tangerine; Midland Region – red lettering on white; Scottish Region – white lettering on pale blue. In a letter to the author, Michael

Bonavia stated that it was likely to have been A.J. White, creator of the British Railways totem, who guided the selection of the regional colours. See The Railway Executive, 'Code of Instructions for Station Name and direction signs', 27 September 1948.

4. Michael Bonavia commented that the Railway Executive 'was continually trying to squash regional independence', and therefore the identities of the former private railway companies. The inception of A.J. White's totem was part of this agenda. While the Railway Executive wanted its own corporate-identity policy, this was suppressed by Sir Brian Robertson, Chairman of the British Transport Commission (1953–62), under direction from the Conservative government. Sir Brian encouraged regional liveries, and consequently a partial return to the separate identities of the former railway companies. This can be seen as a direct reversal of policy by the Labour administration which had nationalized the railways. Only in 1963, after rationalization and a change in structure, did British Railways begin to seek a comprehensive corporate identity. The totem had been largely abandoned by this time.

5. Michael Bonavia to the author, 3 June 1995.

6. Hutchison, *op. cit.* (intr., n.2), p. 13.

7. London Passenger Transport Board, Chairman's minute 338/6/47.

8. Hutchison's findings are recorded in a series of draft reports from August 1948 to January 1949; Hutchison, *op. cit.* (intr., n.2), p. 1.

9. *Ibid.*, p. 1.

10. *Ibid.*, p. 3.

11. *Ibid.*, p. 7.

12. *Ibid.*, pp. 13–14.

13. *Ibid.*, p. 3.

14. On occasion, the symbols would be augmented by the words LONDON and TRANSPORT in the counters, as they had been in 1933.

15. H.F. Hutchison, 'Standardization of Signs' [internal report], 27 August 1948. The chief exception to this rule would be the combined station and headquarters' office entrance at St James's Park. Here, one mast would show the name of the organization, and the other the station name.

16. At stations around the Circle line, these signs were fixed alternately in yellow (Circle) and in green (District) or royal purple (Metropolitan). One notable anomaly is the

pale blue colour used for signs on the Piccadilly line at Holborn, until this colour was transferred to the Victoria line in the mid-1960s.

17. Hutchison, *op. cit.* (ch.2, n.2), p. 20.

18. E.H. Gombrich, *Art and Illusion*, London: Phaidon Press, 1962, p. 197.

19. Michael F. Levey joined London Transport in 1950 as copywriter/researcher. He ran the Copy and Ideas section until the early 1960s, and then supervised its creative output. He became Assistant Publicity Officer in 1965, Publicity Officer in 1975 and resigned c. 1979 to take up the post of Design Manager, retiring in 1981.

20. Sir John Elliot published a letter in the *Daily Express* on 16 December 1954, asking for information relating to the origins of the bulls-eye device. Many retired employees responded with their recollections, several of which offered conflicting assertions of the bulls-eye's origins.

21. J. Elliot with M. Esau, *On and Off the Rails*. London: George Allen & Unwin, 1982, p. 93.

22. Design Research Unit were recruited as consultants to British Railways. The project was led by Misha Black, with a new typeface designed by Jock Kinneir and Margaret Calvert, and a trading symbol by Gerry Barney.

CHAPTER 5

1. J. Holland, *Minerva at fifty: The Jubilee History of the Society of Industrial Artists and Designers 1930 to 1980*. Westerham: Hurtwood Publications, 1980, p. 3.

2. For fuller discussions of Design Research Unit, see J. and A. Blake, *The Practical Idealists: Twenty-five years of designing for industry*. London: Lund Humphries, 1969; and M. Cotton, *Design Research Unit 1942–72*. London: Koenig Books, 2010.

3. N. Dutton, 'Living Design – London Transport'. *Art & Industry*, vol. 41, no. 244, October 1946, pp. 98–123.

4. It is now possible to purchase this garment embellished with the London Underground symbol.

5. 'Inspection of mock-up platform station name bulls-eye signs' [minute 43/10/71]. Notes of Design Panel Meeting no. 67 held on 19 October 1971. The nameboards were displayed as follows: Sloane Square

westbound – red bulls-eyes, white lettering on blue bar, but to new 'roundel' proportions; eastbound – all-red roundel symbol.
6. Specifications for the revised bulls-eye were a 'Bus Red' ring and 'Stewart Blue' (Piccadilly line blue) bar, lettered either *Underground* or *London Transport*. Note 43/10/71 of Design Panel Meeting no. 67 held on 19 October 1971.
7. Michael F. Levey, former London Transport Publicity Officer, in a letter to the author, 13 February 1996.

CHAPTER 6

1. 'Visual identity models: Requirements' [internal briefing notes]. Wolff Olins, 1986.
2. Other coloured bars suggested by Wolff Olins were: green for London Transport International; dark grey for London Transport Advertising; orange for the London Transport Museum; and purple for London Transport Lost Property.
3. Docklands Light Railway vehicles carried the symbol from 1991 to 1992 only, when control of the company passed to the London Docklands Development Corporation. The system is now controlled by Transport for London and carries a modal roundel.
4. Jedco is a team of industrial designers led by John Elson, based in Weybridge, England. See: www.jedco.co.uk

CHAPTER 7

1. London River Services 'owns and operates eight passenger piers on the Thames between Millbank and Greenwich. It also owns the three Woolwich vehicle ferries and their associated terminals and facilities'. For plans on the development of London River Services, see *By the River*: www.tfl.gov.uk/assets/downloads/by-the-river-2009.pdf
2. For an overview of Transport for London Design Standards, see: www.tfl.gov.uk/corporate/media/12523.aspx
3. www.london2012.com/about-us/our-brand
4. www.getaheadofthegames.com/about-us.html

CHAPTER 8

1. art.tfl.gov.uk/about
2. art.tfl.gov.uk/projects/detail/1357
3. art.tfl.gov.uk/projects/current/title/1368. An exhibition was held at Rochelle School, Shoreditch, London, 9–30 October 2008, and selected works have been placed around the system since that time.

CHAPTER 9

1. *Welcome to London: Tourist Information, Underground and Bus Maps 1982*. London Transport and the London Tourist Board, April 1982.
2. Officially called the London Transport Collection of Historic Vehicles, this venue closed on the last day of 1978 in preparation for a move to Covent Garden and the opening of the new London Transport Museum in 1980.
3. *London Transport Shops: Catalogue 1979*. London Transport Publicity Office, March 1979.
4. shop.tfl.gov.uk/design-your-own.html
5. shop.tfl.gov.uk/design-your-own/transport-signs/product/london-underground-silhouette-roundel-signs.html

CHAPTER 10

1. The target nameboard was introduced by John (later Sir John) Elliot, who had secured his post with Southern Railways on the recommendation of the Underground's Lord Ashfield.
2. For example, Ansett Transport Industries of Melbourne, Australia, requested copies of publicity material in 1947, so that they might improve their own marketing activities. TfLCA ref. LT 073/2.
3. The Nyasaland Protectorate has been known as Malawi since 1964.
4. The bus network operated 1932–50 as part of the railway company. Located in Hyderabad State, the railway was nationalized in 1950.

CHAPTER 11

1. The LPTL's Chairman and Founder Jim Blake has stated that 'the group's symbol, though resembling a London Transport [LT] bulls-eye somewhat, was in fact meant to symbolize the venture's proposed transport museum location in Docklands, with a vertical bar through the circle denoting an anchor if I recall correctly'; email to the author, 2 May 2012.
2. www.bbc.co.uk/news/uk-england-london-15695435. The first Occupy LSX camp was established in St Paul's Churchyard, London, 15 October 2011, and left the location 28 February 2012. See: www.occupylondon.org.uk

CONCLUSION

1. www.tfl.gov.uk/corporate/media/12523.aspx
2. shop.tfl.gov.uk/design-your-own.html and www.ltmuseumshop.co.uk/exclusive-and-vintage.html
3. www.thecoca-colacompany.com/heritage/ourheritage.html
4. www.london2012.com and www.wolffolins.com/work/london-2012
5. *The Mayor's Rail Vision – Investing in Rail Services in London*. Greater London Authority, February 2012. See: www.lgcplus.com/Journals/2012/02/06/p/h/j/London-rail.pdf

PRIMARY SOURCES

CRAFTS STUDY CENTRE, UNIVERSITY FOR THE CREATIVE ARTS, FARNHAM: EDWARD JOHNSTON COLLECTION & ARCHIVE (CSC)

Collection boxes: 8, 9, 11, 12, 13; Archive Box CL29/EJArch 3.
Collection objects: C.86.125; C.86.128.i–ii; C.86.129.ii–iii; C.86.130.i; C.86.134.i–v.
Archive papers: 2/122–166.

LONDON METROPOLITAN ARCHIVES

ACC/1297/CXEH/01/002 Board Meetings File 1900–1909.
ACC/1297/LER/01/006 General Meeting Minutes of the Great Northern, Piccadilly and Brompton Railway 1903–1910.
ACC/1297/LGOC/01/031 Board Meetings File 1905–1906.
ACC/1297/MDR/01/010 Board and General Meetings File 1907–1911.
LMA/4418/01/004 Garnier and Company Limited: order forms, price lists and sales brochures for souvenirs, including sample keyring.

BOOKS AND JOURNALS

An introduction to the London Transport Buses visual identity. London Transport Buses, October 1994.
Architecture and Design. London Regional Transport: Department of Architecture and Design, July 1985.
Carr, H.T., *London Transport Totem: its origin and design* [private manuscript], December 1954.
Carr–Edwards Report 1938 with amendments to 1948. London Transport Executive, Chief Public Relations Officer, 10 December 1948.
Changing Stations: A review of recent London Underground Station Design by LUL's Architectural Services and their Consultants. London: LUL Architectural Services, 1993.
Clarke, H.L., *Bar and Circle* [typescript]. c. 1974.
Corporate Identity Basic Rules and Specifications: 1. The Roundel and Logotype. London Transport, n.d.
Design Committee meeting minutes December 1964–December 1974 (file 104). London Transport Board.
Design Research Unit, *Draft Content of Report: London Transport Design Survey (file 945).* May 1971.
Edward Johnston Collection and Archive: catalogue with revisions dated 8 November 1988. Bath: Holburne Museum, 1988.
How to use and protect the intellectual property rights of London Transport. London Transport, n.d.
How to use the London Transport Corporate Identity. London Transport, 1990.
Howes, Justin, *Edward Johnston: a Catalogue of the Crafts Study Centre Collection & Archive.* Bath: Crafts Study Centre, 1987.
Hutchison, Harold F., *Standard Signs* [internal publication]. London Transport Executive, 11 October 1951.
Hutchison, Harold F., *Publicity relations at London Transport.* c. 1952.
Latchford, A.L., *Winged Wheels and Bullseyes.* London Transport Press and Publications Office, Technical and Press Section, 13 December 1954.
Latham, The Rt. Hon. Lord, *Design in London Transport* [a paper given at the International Design Congress, Festival of Britain], 1951.
London Buses Corporate Identity Manual. London Buses Limited, 1987.
London Buses Roundel [guidelines for correct use of the roundel]. London Buses Limited, 1987.
London Passenger Transport Board. *Fifth Annual Report and Statement of Accounts and Statistics for the Year ended 30 June 1938.* London: London Passenger Transport Board, 27 October 1938.
London Transport Design Manual. London Transport Executive Publicity Office, January 1978.
London Underground heritage signing handbook. London Underground Limited, March 1993.
London Underground Limited colour standards. London Underground Limited, 1991.
London Underground roundel guidelines. London Underground Limited, February 1997.
Piccadilly line – Western Extension: Review of first year's working. London Passenger Transport Board: Office of General Manager (Rlys.), 10 March 1934.
Publicity Office Letters Register. London Passenger Transport Board, c. 1935.
Railways and Roads Standard Signs Manual. London Transport Executive, August 1948.
Register of Letters, Patents, Registered Designs, Trade Marks and Licences. Underground Electric Railway Company of London Ltd, London & Suburban Traction Company Ltd and Allied Companies, n.d.
Standard Signs, London Transport (Railways). London Passenger Transport Board, March 1938, with appendices to 26 June 1938 and 19 June 1947.
Thompson, Vera (ed. Cliff Wadsworth), *Nothing too large! Nothing too small! The Story of Garnier & Company, Limited. Manufacturers of Vitreous Enamelled Steel Signs in Willesden Since 1898.* n.p.: Vera Thompson, 1998. Proof copy of manuscript.
Transport in London – Biographical details of Prominent Persons [third draft]. London Transport Group Archive, June 1995.
Victoria Line – some propositions for the consideration of the Design Panel. London Transport Board Publicity Office, 2 October 1963.

FURTHER READING

100 Years, 100 Artists, 100 Works of Art:
Learning guide. London: Art on the
Underground, 2008.

Badsey-Ellis, Anthony, *The Hampstead Tube:*
A history of the first 100 years. Harrow:
Capital Transport, 2007.

Banham, Reyner, *Theory and Design in the*
First Machine Age [first published 1960].
New York: Praeger Publishers, 2nd edn,
2nd printing, 1970.

Barman, C., *The Writing on the Wall* [internal
publication]. London Transport
Underground Railways, 1938.

Barman, C., *The Man Who Built London*
Transport – a biography of Frank Pick.
Newton Abbot: David & Charles, 1979.

Barnes, Richard, *Mods!*, London: Eel Pie
Publishing, 1979.

Baynes, Ken, *Industrial Design & the*
Community. London: Lund Humphries,
1967.

Blacker, Ken, *The London Trolleybus Volume 1*
1931–45. Harrow Weald: Capital Transport
Publishing, 2002.

Blacker, Ken, *The London Trolleybus Volume 2*
1946–62. Harrow Weald: Capital Transport
Publishing, 2004.

Blake, Avril, *Misha Black.* London: The Design
Council, 1984.

Blake, Jim and Jonathan James, *Northern*
Wastes: The Story of the Uncompleted
Northern Line Extensions. London:
Platform Ten Productions/LPTL, 1987.

Blake, John and Avril Blake, *The Practical*
Idealists: Twenty-five years of designing
for industry. London: Lund Humphries,
1969.

Bonavia, M.R., *The Birth of British Rail.*
London: George Allen & Unwin, 1979.

Bonavia, M.R., *British Rail: The First 25 Years.*
Newton Abbot: David & Charles, 1981.

Brennand, Dave and Richard Furness, *The*
Book of British Railways Station totems.
Stroud: Sutton Publishing, 2002.

Caplan, D. and G. Stewart, *British Trademarks*
and Symbols. London: Peter Owen, 1966.

Carter, Ernest F., *Britain's Railway liveries –*
colours, crests and linings, 1825–1948.
London: Burke, 1952.

Clarke, Hedley, *Underground Bullseyes*
1972–2000. Colchester: Connor & Butler,
2007.

Collins, Paul, *Tramway Memories London.*
Hersham: Ian Allan Publishing, 2005.

Collins, Stanley Guildford and Terence
Cooper (eds), *The Wheels Used to Talk to Us:*
A London Tramwayman Remembers.
Sheffield: Tallis Publishing, 1977.

Cotton, Michelle, *Design Research Unit*
1942–72. London: Koenig Books, 2010.

Darling, Elizabeth, *Re-forming Britain:*
Narratives of modernity before
reconstruction. London: Routledge, 2007.

Day, John R. and John Reed, *The Story of*
London's Underground. n.p.: Capital
Transport Publishing, 2010.

Demuth, Tim, *The Spread of London's*
Underground. Harrow Weald: Capital
Transport Publishing, 2003.

Dormer, Peter, *Design since 1945.* London:
Thames and Hudson, 1993.

Dow, George, *Railway Heraldry and other*
insignia. Newton Abbot: David & Charles,
1973.

Dreyfuss, Henry, *Symbol Sourcebook.* New
York: McGraw-Hill, 1972.

Eckersley, Tom, *Poster Design* [How To Do It
Series 50]. London: The Studio, 1954.

Elliot, Sir John, in association with Michael
Esau, *On and Off the Rails.* London: George
Allen & Unwin, 1982.

Foley, John, *The Guinness Encyclopedia of Signs*
& Symbols. Enfield: Guinness Publishing,
1993.

Froggatt, David J., *Railway Buttons, Badges &*
Uniforms. Shepperton: Ian Allan, 1986.

Froggatt, David J., *Railway Buttons, Badges &*
Uniforms: Supplement 1. Lincoln: privately
published, August 1989.

Games, Naomi, *Poster Journeys: Abram Games*
and London Transport. Harrow Weald:
Capital Transport Publishing, 2008.

Garfield, Simon, *Just My Type: a book about*
fonts (first published 2010). London:
Profile Books, 2011.

Garland, Ken, *Mr Beck's Underground Map.*
Harrow Weald: Capital Transport
Publishing, 1994.

Generations: Celebrating 50 years of Caribbean
recruitment. Transport for London Group
Publishing, 2006.

Glancey, Jonathan, *Douglas Scott.* London:
The Design Council, 1988.

Gombrich, E.H., *Art and Illusion* (first
published 1959). London: Phaidon Press,
1962.

Graves, Charles, *London Transport Carried On:*
An account of London at war, 1939–1945.
Westminster: London Passenger Transport
Board, 1947.

Green, Oliver and John Reed, *The London*
Transport Golden Jubilee Book 1933–1983.
London: The Daily Telegraph, 1983.

Haresnape, Brian, *British Rail 1948–83: A*
Journey by Design. Shepperton: Ian Allan,
1979.

Haresnape, Brian, *Railway Liveries 1923–1947.*
Shepperton: Ian Allan, 1989.

Harley, Robert J., *London Tramway Twilight*
1949–1952. Harrow Weald: Capital
Transport, 2000.

Horne, Mike, *The Last Link: The First 30*
Years of The Hampstead Tube 1907–1937.
London/Alton: London Underground
Ltd (Northern Line)/Nebulous Books,
2007.

Howes, Justin, *Edward Bawden: A Retrospective*
Survey. Bath: Combined Arts, 1988.

Howes, Justin, *Johnston's Underground Type.*
Harrow Weald: Capital Transport
Publishing, 2000.

Hughes-Stanton, Corin, 'Design
Management: Pioneering Policies'. *Design*,
May 1965, pp. 3745.

Hutchison, Harold F., *Art For All. An exhibition*
of posters & their originals produced by
London Transport 1908–1949. London: Arts
Council of Great Britain, 1949.

Hutchison, Harold F. (intr. James Laver), *Art for All: London Transport Posters 1908–1949*. London: Art and Technics, 1949.

Hutchison, Harold F., *Visitor's London: An alphabetical reference book for the visitor to London who wishes also to see something of London's countryside*. London Transport, 1954.

Hutchison, Harold F., *Design & Public Taste* (reprinted from Design and Industries Association Year Book 1955).

Johnston, Priscilla (Priscilla Gill), *Edward Johnston*. London: Faber and Faber, 1959.

Kinneir, Jock, *Words and Buildings*. London: The Architectural Press, 1980.

Klein, Naomi, *No Space No Choice No Jobs No Logo* (first published in the UK 2000). London: Flamingo, 2001.

Kuwayama, Yasaburo, *Trademarks & Symbols Volume 2: Symbolical Designs*. New York: Van Nostrand Reinhold Company, 1973.

Latchford, A.L. and H. Pollins, *London General: The story of the London Bus 1856–1956*. London: London Transport, 1956.

Lawrence, David, *London Transport Cap Badges*. Harrow Weald: Capital Transport Publishing, 1989.

Lawrence, David, *Underground Architecture*. Harrow Weald: Capital Transport Publishing, 1994.

Lawrence, David, *Bright Underground Spaces*. Harrow Weald: Capital Transport Publishing, 2008.

Lehner, Ernst, *The Picture Book of Symbols*. New York: Wm. Penn Publishing Corporation, 1956.

Levey, Michael F., *London Transport Posters*. London: Phaidon/London Transport, 1976.

London's Underground, *London Town & Country: a guide for the visitor and the resident*. London: St. Catherine's Press, 1928.

MacCarthy, Fiona, *Eric Gill*. London: Faber and Faber, 1989.

Making a mark: The development of London Transport's Visual Identity. London Transport, 1990.

Marshall, Prince, *Wheels of London*. London: The Sunday Times Magazine, 1972.

Olins, Wally, *Wally Olins On B®and*. London: Thames & Hudson, 2003.

Olins, Wally, *Wally Olins: The Brand Handbook*. London: Thames & Hudson, 2008.

Peters, George H., *The Plimsoll Line*. Chichester: Barry Rose, 1975.

Read, Herbert, *Art & Industry: The Principles of Industrial Design* (first published 1934). London: Faber and Faber, 1966.

Rosen, Ben, *The Corporate Search for Visual Identity*. New York: Van Nostrand Reinhold Company, 1970.

Saler, Michael T., *The Avant-Garde in Interwar England: Medieval Modernism and the London Underground*. Oxford/New York: Oxford University Press, 1999.

Schaffer, Frank, *The New Town Story* (first published 1970). London: Paladin, 1972.

Schleger, Pat, *Zero: Hans Schleger – a life of design*. Aldershot: Lund Humphries, 2001.

Seuss, Juergen, Gerold Dommermuth and Hans Maier, *London pop gesehen*. Hanover: Fackelträger-Verlag Schmidt-Küster, 1969.

Shepherd, Walter, *Shepherd's Glossary of Graphic Signs and Symbols*. London: J.M. Dent, 1971.

Thin Cities. London: Art on the Underground, 2008.

Tom Eckersley OBE, RGI, AGI: His Graphic Work. London: London College of Printing, 1994.

Werkman, Casper J., *Trademarks – Their Creation, Psychology and Perception*. Harlow: Longman Group, 1974.

Year 2107: The future of London Transport [A set of four A3 prints].

Zero: Hans Schleger – a life of design 1898–1976 (exhibition catalogue). An exhibition at The London Institute Gallery Mayfair, 15 February to 14 March 2002.

WEB RESOURCES

Abram Games: www.abramgames.com

Art on the Underground: art.tfl.gov.uk

The Edward Johnston Foundation: www.ejf.org.uk

London Transport e-plates, bus-stop flags, maps and a London Transport bibliography by Alan Gryfe: www.eplates.info/maps

London Transport Museum: www.ltmuseum.co.uk/collections

London Transport Museum Shop: www.ltmuseumshop.co.uk

Mike Rohde's Metrobits.org, Metro Logos: www.mic-ro.com/metro/metrologos-static.html

Transport for London logo requests: www.tfl.gov.uk/tfl/corporate/media/logos/default.asp

Wolff Olins: www.wolffolins.com

INDEX

PICTURE CREDITS

All the images reproduced in this book are © Transport for London, courtesy of the London Transport Museum, unless stated otherwise below:

A Salt & Battery, New York	page 153, third row, centre
Commissioned by Art on the Underground, © Transport for London	pages 132, 135, 136, 137 (left), 138, 139, 140, 141
Commissioned by Art on the Underground, © Olivia Plender	page 137 (right)
Author's collection	pages 11, 12, 26, 30 (middle), 46, 47, 52 (lower), 57 (upper), 62, 64, 65 (upper), 68, 69, 72 (left lower), 81, 85, 86, 87, 88, 89, 90, 95, 99 (upper), 100, 101, 104, 108, 109 (upper left, lower right), 110, 111, 119, 120, 121, 123 (lower), 124, 125, 134, 142, 143, 144, 145, 147 (upper), 148, 149, 150, 151, 153 (third and bottom rows), 158, 159, 161 (Sgt. Peppers, Eindhoven), 161 (Hard Rock Cafe)
© David Batchelor, photo Daisy Hutchison	page 133
BlissHome, www.blisshome.co.uk	page 147 (lower)
Tom Eckersley	page 112
Justin Howes/Capital Transport Publishing	pages 31, 48
© Andrew and Angela Johnston/ Crafts Study Centre, University for the Creative Arts	pages 42, 43
Daniel Kirkdorffer © 2006	page 161 (Optical Underground, San Francisco)
Mark Moore (S-Express) and Arista BMG Eurodisc Ltd	page 157 (second row)
Modern World Gallery, Brighton, www.modernworldgallery.com	page 156
Nestlé UK Ltd	page 153 (second row, right)
Nissan Europe N.V.	page 153 (second row, left and centre)
© David Samuel	page 154
Wolff Olins	page 116

From the Annie Mole photostream on flickr.com:
Jon Allen (page 161, Abbey Road, Seoul); Anne (page 161, Playground, Naples); Lisa A. (page 161, Glass Plus LLC, Middlesboro); Ian (page 161, Penny Lane, Dortmund); Joana (page 161, Laekjargata, Reykjavik); Carolyn Jones (page 157, Waterloo Records, Austin); Julio (page 161, Electrica Procables, Tijuana); Leo (page 161, Underground Lighting, Antwerp); Geoff Marshall (page 161, Charlotte Street, Ashville); Mark Morton (page 161, Lunch Station, Sheffield); Pete Stean (page 161, Sex-Shop & Kino, Berlin); Anno Superstar (page 161, Record Hunter, Stockholm); John T. (page 161, Railroad Transport, Adelaide); Tina Threadgill (page 161, Bombay Grill, Albuquerque); Drew White (page 161, Pub, Sao Paulo); Michael Windsor (page 161, Camden Town, Gdansk).

ACKNOWLEDGEMENTS

A really hearty thank you to everyone who has contributed to this project – at Laurence King Publishing: Philip Cooper, Felicity Maunder and Zoe Foster, with the assistance of David Pearson, Nicky Barneby and Ian McDonald; at Transport for London: the Corporate Design team, past and current; at London Underground: Mike Brown, Linda Thompson, Mike Ashworth; at the London Transport Museum: Helen Grove, Martin Harrison-Putnam, Sam Mullins, Simon Murphy, Wendy Neville, Michael Walton, Caroline Warhurst and David Worthington; at Transport for London Corporate Archives: Stephanie Rousseau; at Capital Transport Publishing: James Whiting for the initial publication and proposal to republish; at Art on the Underground: Tamsin Dillon and Rebecca Bell.

I would also like to thank the following individuals and organizations for their assistance and support in creating this book, and for permission to reproduce images:

Nicky Perry, A Salt & Battery
Giles Bartleet, Bacardi-Martini Ltd
David Batchelor
Gary Bayfield
Bryce Beaumont
Richard Bevington
Ashley Birch
Jim Blake
Dr Michael R. Bonavia
Sidney Boulonois
Alan Burcher
Burnham Signs (Onyx) Ltd
Vivien Castle
Dr Hedley Clarke
Andrew Colebourne
Jean Vacher, Collections Manager at the Crafts Study Centre, University for the Creative Arts, Farnham
Charlie Crouch
Design Research Unit
Tom and Paul Eckersley

W.P.N. Edwards
John Fairbrother
William Fenton
Innes Ferguson
June Fraser
Stan and Val Friedman
Naomi Games
Ken Garland
Henry Gibbs
Annie Mole, Going Underground
Professor Sir Ernst Gombrich
Oliver Green
Philip Greenslade
Cliff Hall
Mike Harris
Andrew and Angela Johnston
Chris Ludlow, co-founder, Henrion, Ludlow & Schmidt
M.F. Higson
Derek Hodgson, Hodgson Associates
Justin Howes
Corin Hughes-Stanton
L.J. Hutchison
Charles Hutton
Cornelia de Uphaugh and Maria Eisl, Stephen Jones Millinery
Scott King
Daniel Kirkdorffer
Lin Downes, Kate Osborne, Rachel Pownall and Nicola Salliss, Knight's Park Library
Mike Lawrence
Michael F. Levey
The London Metropolitan Archives
Carole Love
Ian Maclean
Eline McGeorge
Marta Marcé
Julian de Takats, Mother Tongue Records
Jennifer Tobias, The Museum of Modern Art Library
Christopher Nell
Sarah Dixon, Nestlé UK Ltd
Nissan Europe N.V.
Jim Blake, North London Transport Society

Brian Pask
Olivia Plender
Harry Ralph
Kim Rennie
Ken Rutland
Alan Kirby-Woolmore, Scala UK
Pat Schleger, Hans Schleger Associates
Splash Promotions
J.K. Wright, Strathclyde Passenger Transport Underground Railway
David F. Taylor
Bev Thomas
Vera Thompson
Jim Baker, Andy Cleverley, Christine Cushing, Brenda Davis, Steve Randle, Khush Singh and Fiona Toye, Toye & Co.
Charlie Tweed
Anne Tyrrell, MBE, Anne Tyrrell Design
Reginald Wakelin
Jim Westgate
Michael Wickham
Cliff Wadsworth, Willesden Local History Society
Wolff Olins Ltd

David Lawrence, Globe Town, 2013